Shelmerdine's Introduction to Latin:
A Workbook

Shelmerdine's Introduction to Latin: A Workbook

Ed DeHoratius
Wayland High School

Contents

The study of Latin requires a ratio of knowledge and understanding. Perhaps at the beginning of your study, you will acquire more knowledge than understanding, but as your Latin expands that ratio will skew as much to understanding as to knowledge. This book strives to help you achieve that balance. On the one hand, it focuses on knowledge of Latin: do you know forms, endings, vocabulary? On the other hand, it develops your understanding of Latin, asking you to explain choices you made when translating, or presenting ambiguous situations that force you to use context to answer. Both of these approaches are essential to developing your facility with Latin.

The structure of this book maintains the structure of your textbook. The chapters and the section numbers remain the same so that you can quickly find exercises in the workbook that correspond to the grammar of the textbook. The vocabulary of your textbook is also maintained, so that within the exercises there should be no words that you have not already studied (with some exceptions that are glossed for you). The vocabulary will, however, not come exclusively from the current chapter; forcing you to recall important words from previous lists goes a long way to helping you remember those words. In addition, each chapter contains at its end a derivatives exercise that allows you to draw connections between the Latin words that you are learning and the English words that they have yielded.

Grammar exercises form the bulk of this book. Each exercise was tailored to a specific grammatical topic with two questions in mind: what will help you better understand that topic? and what will help you avoid common mistakes associated with that topic? In addition, multiple exercises on the same topic are included to allow for either graded repetition, i.e. repetition that becomes more difficult as it progresses, or differentiated instruction, providing both those with an initial understanding of a topic and those with a more advanced understanding exercises appropriate for their needs. Each exercise includes a minimum of ten questions, some with as many as twenty, and exercises that focus on English grammar as an avenue to understanding Latin grammar are included as well.

In the end, this book will be one of many tools at your disposal. It is my hope that it will provide another way for you to develop and better understand Latin. Perhaps most important for you as a Latin learner is to take your time and not forget to think questions through. Many answers will not be immediately obvious or may seem correct when in reality they are not. But it is the discipline and focus that Latin requires that make it such a rewarding language to learn.

- differentiated instruction, i.e. approaching grammatical topics from multiple pedagogical approaches: multiple choice, fill-in, generation, etc.
- keyed to Shelmerdine's sections for direct connection to whatever is being taught
- all vocab used in exercises from Shelmerdine's vocabulary lists; words chosen are from both current and prior chapters, and focus on words used with higher frequency
- prepared by a 15-year teacher

- derivatives work for each vocab list included
- completed example included for each exercise to better facilitate successful independent work
- Includes work with English sentences and grammar to illustrate connections between English and Latin grammar
- English sentences, when used, about Roman topics for (brief) cultural introductions
- Some exercises include 'explain your answer' prompts to focus on the articulation of understanding rather than the demonstration of knowledge
- Includes a minimum of 10 questions per exercise to provide enough variety and repetition
- two graphic exercises (chaps. 4 & 7; might not be a talking point but these might be good to show prospective buyers)
- later chapters include authentic Latin when work becomes less rote and more conceptual or big-picture
- shuffled noun & pronoun paradigms (i.e. not in the traditional nom., gen., dat., etc. order) to force active recall of forms

CHAPTER 1

SECTIONS 2-7: TERMS MATCHING. In the left column are terms from sections 2-7. In the right column are definitions. Write the letter of the definition in the blank to the left of the term. The definitions are taken directly from the textbook; define as many terms as possible without referring to the textbook.

_____ 1. verb

_____ 2. noun

_____ 3. adjective

_____ 4. adverb

_____ 5. preposition

_____ 6. pronoun

_____ 7. conjunction

_____ 8. interjection

_____ 9. subject

_____ 10. direct object

_____ 11. intransitive verb

_____ 12. transitive verb

_____ 13. conjugation

_____ 14. stem

_____ 15. personal ending

_____ 16. number

_____ 17. tense

_____ 18. voice

_____ 19. mood

_____ 20. infinitive

_____ 21. principal part

_____ 22. indicative

_____ 23. complementary infinitive

a. the person or thing a sentence is about

b. usually modifies a verb, giving information about time, place, manner or degree

c. singular or plural

d. carries information about who the subject of the verb is

e. takes a direct object

f. contain the verbs stems on which all other forms are built

g. whether the verb is a simple statement or question, or a command

h. expresses existence, action, or occurrence

i. substitutes for a noun, referring to something without naming it

j. names a person, place or thing, (including an idea or a quality

k. completes the meaning of another verb

l. does not take a direct object

m. connects words or groups of words

n. carries the meaning of a verb and its characteristic vowel

o. person or thing that receives the action of the verb directly

p. verb form not limited by a personal ending

q. four regular groups for verbs

r. connects a noun or pronoun to another word and shows a relationship between the two

s. when an action happens

t. adds to (modifies) the meaning of a noun or pronoun to specify a quality

u. whether the subject is doing the action or receiving the action

v. makes simple statements and asks simple questions

w. an exclamation

SECTION 4: TRANSITIVE VS. INTRANSITIVE. [The following sentences are those found in Exercise 4 in the Textbook.] Identify whether the following sentences are transitive or intransitive by placing a T or an I in the blank to the left of the sentence. (Review section 4, pp.6-7, in the Textbook if necessary.)

T   Fēmina nautam videt.

_____ 1. Agricola labōrat.

_____ 2. Agricolam vocāmus.

_____ 3. Fēmina rosam habet.

_____ 4. Tacētis.

_____ 5. Nauta aquam videt?

_____ 6. Fēminam docent.

_____ 7. Labōrāre optās?

_____ 8. Fortūna nautam iuvat.

_____ 9. Tacēre dēbeō.

_____ 10. Fāmam amāmus.

SECTION 5: VERB NUMBER CHANGE. [The following verbs are those found in Excerise 1 in the Textbook.] Change the number of the following forms and write the new Latin form in the blank. Do not translate; focus instead on changing the form and understanding its new meaning.

superāmus   superō

1. optat   _____

2. vident   _____

3. habēmus   _____

4. labōrātis   _____

5. timeō   _____

6. vocās   _____

7. tacēs   _____

8. iacētis   _____

9. superant   _____

10. iuvāmus   _____

SECTION 6: PRINCIPAL PARTS. Identify the following verb forms by their principal part by writing a one, two, three, or four in the blank to the left of the form; if the form is not a principal part, write 'N' in the blank. (You should only identify a form as a principal part if it is that principal part exactly as it is written in the vocabulary on p.11 of your textbook; forms derived from principal parts should be labeled 'N'.) Review the Principal Parts section on pp.8-9 of your textbook if necessary.

4   superātus

_____ 1. vocāvī

_____ 2. superās

_____ 3. doctus

_____ 4. timēre

_____ 5. dēbuērunt

_____ 6. optātus

_____ 7. habitō

_____ 8. tacē-

_____ 9. videō

_____ 10. iacuī

_____ 11. labōrātis

_____ 12. laudāvī

_____ 13. vocātī

_____ 14. iuvant

_____ 15. amāmus

SECTION 7: INDICATIVE AND INFINITIVE FORMS. Identify the following forms as indicative or infinitive by placing an 'N' (indicative) or an 'F' (infinitive) in the blanks to the left of the forms.

N   timent

_____ 1. superāre   _____ 4. laborō   _____ 7. habēmus

_____ 2. laudant   _____ 5. docēre   _____ 8. amāre

_____ 3. iuvāre   _____ 6. vocās   _____ 9. tacet

SECTION 7: COMPLEMENTARY INFINITIVE. Write the infinitive form for the italicized English in the first blank to complete the Latin sentence. Then translate the sentence in the second blank. When translating the sentences, focus on the ending on the non-infinitive verb for your subject; review the personal endings on p.7 in the textbook, and the indicative forms on p.8 if necessary.

Optāmus to see.   vidēre   **We want to see.**

                          LATIN INFINITIVE   TRANSLATION

1. Dēbet to be silent.   _____   _____

2. Optō to teach.   _____   _____

3. Dēbēs to help.   _____   _____

4. Optātis to call.   _____   _____

5. Dēbēmus to lie (down).   _____   _____

6. Optant to see.   _____   _____

VOCABULARY: DERIVATIVES. Write the English word from the list below, derived from one of the Chapter 1 vocabulary words, that completes the following English sentences in the first blank, and write the Latin word from which it is derived in the second blank. The blank for the English word has been divided into individual blanks for each letter for assistance.

defamation	fortunate	nautical	amatory	debit
docent	adjacent	belabored	collaboration	laudable
taciturn	tacit	visage	evoke	irrevocable

1. The _____ glance from the young man signaled his interest from across the room.

— — — — — — —   _____

2. After reading what the tabloid had written about him, the celebrity discussed a _____ suit with his lawyer.

— — — — — — — — — —   _____

3. The twins had a _____ understanding; they didn't need to speak to know what the other was thinking.

— — — — —   _____

4. She knew that she was _____ to have found her keys; she hadn't put them where she normally does.

— — — — — — — — —   _____

5. The trend was _____; once they lost three games in a row, they lost the rest of the games of their season.

— — — — — — — — — —   _____

6. His efforts were _____: his opponent was taller and stronger, but the shorter player still gave him a good game.

— — — — — — —   _____

7. Since these seats are taken, why don't we sit in the _____ ones; they're just as close but a little farther over.

— — — — — — —   _____

8. He didn't love the _____ theme of the decoration of the house: brass fittings, navy blue, and hurricane flags just weren't his style.

— — — — — — —   _____

9. The smell of basil tends to _____ memories of Italy because of its ubiquity in Italian cooking.

— — — — —   _____

10. Since I lost my credit card, I'll have to use my _____ card, even though it will pull directly from my bank account, which is depleted.

— — — — —   _____

11. For this project, you will work in _____; each group of five has two weeks to finish the project.

— — — — — — — — — — —   _____

12. The _____ at the art museum was very good; she knew her stuff and could communicate the information well to the student group.

— — — — — —   _____

13. The judge's _____ betrayed his frustration with the prosecutor; he could see it from the way she looked at him.

— — — — — —   _____

14. His girlfriend's father appeared _____ and gruff (he scowled a lot and didn't say much), but she assured him he would loosen up.

— — — — — — — —   _____

15. Even though the teacher _____ the point, the student understood how angry she was.

— — — — — — — —   _____

VOCABULARY: DEFINITIONS. In the left column are vocabulary words from Chapter 1. In the right column are definitions. Write the letter of the definition in the blank to the left of the term. The definitions are taken directly from the textbook.

_____ 1. doceō, -ēre		a. to fear, be afraid
_____ 2. iuvō, -āre		b. rose
_____ 3. rosa, -ae		c. to call; name
_____ 4. videō, -ēre		d. to choose, desire, wish for
_____ 5. fortūna, -ae		e. farmer
_____ 6. labōrō, -āre		f. to lie (e.g. on the ground)
_____ 7. vocō, -āre		g. to overcome, conquer, surpass
_____ 8. iaceō, -ēre		h. to love
_____ 9. amō, -āre		i. to praise
_____ 10. timeō, -ēre		j. to teach
_____ 11. aqua, -ae		k. water
_____ 12. agricola, -ae		l. sailor
_____ 13. superō, -āre		m. to help; please
_____ 14. fāma, -ae		n. woman
_____ 15. habeō, -ēre		o. to see
_____ 16. laudō, -āre		p. fame, report, reputation; rumor
_____ 17. optō, -āre		q. to have, hold; consider
_____ 18. debeō, -ēre		r. to owe; to be obligated to
_____ 19. fēmina, -ae		s. to work, strive
_____ 20. nauta, -ae		t. chance, luck, fortune

SECTION 8B: CASE USES. In the sentences below, both Latin and English, underline the subject (nominative) and circle the direct object (accusative). The first three are translations of each other; the remaining are separate. Be prepared to explain how you decided which noun was which.

1a. Dominus puerum terret.

1b. The master scares the boy.

2a. Puer puellam videt.

2b. The boy sees the girl.

3a. Vir cōnsilium dubitat.

3b. The man doubts the plan.

4. Nātūra puerōs terret.

11. The friend shouts to the boys.

5. Puellae locum dubitant.

12. War requires advice.

6. Agrī virōs terrent.

13. Nature teaches the girls.

7. Puerī et puellae litterās dubitant.

14. The men call their master.

8. Nātūram et litterās virī superant.

15. The master fears the kingdom.

9. Agrōs agricolae laudant.

16. The boy and the girl doubt the gifts.

10. Animum fortūna iuvat.

SECTION 9: BASE FORMATION. Write the bases of the following nouns in the blanks next to them. (The nouns are taken from the vocabulary list on p.20 of the textbook.)

      dōnum, dōnī   **dōn-**

1. amīcus, amīcī _____

6. ager, agrī _____

2. nātūra, nātūrae _____

7. puella, puellae _____

3. rēgnum, rēgnī _____

8. vir, virī _____

4. littera, litterae _____

9. locus, locī _____

5. dominus, dominī _____

10. puer, puerī _____

SECTION 10: GENDER. Identify the Latin gender of the following nouns in the first blank, and their corresponding English gender in the second blank. You should know gender as part of your vocabulary studying, but you may refer to the vocabulary list on p.20 of the textbook if necessary. Note that with some nouns the Latin gender and English gender will match, while with other nouns it will not. (You may abbreviate your genders with M, F, and N.)

bellum, -ī   **LG: neuter**   **EG: neuter**

	Lat. Gend.	Eng. Gend.		Lat. Gend.	Eng. Gend.
1. vir, -ī	_____	_____	6. littera, -ae	_____	_____
2. puella, -ae	_____	_____	7. dōnum, -ī	_____	_____
3. animus, -ī	_____	_____	8. ager, -rī	_____	_____
4. dominus, -ī	_____	_____	9. nātūra, -ae	_____	_____
5. rēgnum, -ī	_____	_____	10. puer, -ī	_____	_____

SECTIONS 10-13: USING THE DICTIONARY. Using the glossary for words beginning with the letters G and H, page 322, choose ten nouns and write the nominative form in the left-most column (this is the form under which the noun is listed) and write the genitive form of the noun in the next column. Then write the gender and declension in the corresponding columns. (Not all nouns in this section will be first or second declension nouns; if you don't yet know the declension, write a question mark in the 'Declension' column.)

Nominative	Genitive	Gender	Declension
1. _____	_____	_____	_____
2. _____	_____	_____	_____
3. _____	_____	_____	_____
4. _____	_____	_____	_____
5. _____	_____	_____	_____
6. _____	_____	_____	_____
7. _____	_____	_____	_____
8. _____	_____	_____	_____
9. _____	_____	_____	_____
10. _____	_____	_____	_____

SECTIONS 12-13: CASE ENDINGS OF THE 1ST AND 2ND DECLENSIONS. Complete the following chart as best as possible from memory. When necessary, use the paradigms on pp.15-17 for reference.

	nātūra, -ae	dominus, -ī	bellum, -ī
		singular	
genitive			
ablative			
nominative			
accusative			
dative			
		plural	
dative			
accusative			
nominative			
ablative			
genitive			

SECTIONS 12-13: IDENTIFYING CASES. Change the number of the following nouns, i.e. make the singular nouns plural and the plural nouns singular. Keep the case the same. When more than one possibility exists, more than one blank has been provided.

puellīs   **puellae**   **puellā**

1. litteram _____

2. nātūrae _____

_____

_____

3. cōnsilium _____

4. animī _____

_____

5. bellō _____

6. regnīs _____

7. puellā _____

8. puellārum _____

9. dominōs _____

10. puer _____

11. cōnsiliōrum _____

12. dominum _____

SECTIONS 12-13: IDENTIFYING CASES. Circle the correct noun from the nouns in parentheses to complete these sentences, and translate them in the blank provided.

Puella _____ (virō, virum, vir) terret.   **The girl terrifies the man.**

1. Agricola _____ (agrōs, ager, agrī) dubitat.   _____

2. Aquam _____ (nautās, nauta, nautā) amat.   _____

3. Dominī _____ (vir, virōs, virī) vocant.   _____

4. Rēgnum _____ (agrōs, agrī, agrīs) habet.   _____

5. Puer et puella _____ (dominus, dominōs, dominō) ōrant. _____

6. Dominum _____ (nātūram, nātūra, nātūrae) dubitat. _____

7. Virī _____ (bellum, bellō, bellī) dubitant.   _____

8. Puerī _____ (dōna, dōnōrum, dōnīs) habent.   _____

9. _____ (Puella, Puellae, Puellam) cōnsilium habet. _____

10. _____ (Amīcī, Amīcum, Amīcus) locum videt.   _____

VOCABULARY: DEFINITIONS. Match the vocabulary words from Chapter 2 with the definitions on the right by writing the letter of the definition in the blank.

_____ 1. regnum, -ī   a. nature
_____ 2. littera, -ae   b. plan, advice
_____ 3. terreō, -ēre   c. but
_____ 4. cōnsilium, -ī   d. kingdom, royal power
_____ 5. bellum, -ī   e. to pray, beg, beg for
_____ 6. –que   f. girl
_____ 7. ōrō, -āre   g. (cultivated) field; countryside
_____ 8. puella, -ae   h. to dare
_____ 9. animus, -ī   i. letter (of the alphabet); pl. letter, literature
_____ 10. locus, -ī   j. place, position
_____ 11. dubitō, -āre   k. war
_____ 12. sed   l. master, lord
_____ 13. vir, -ī   m. and
_____ 14. ager, -rī   n. and
_____ 15. nātūra, -ae   o. man; hero; husband
_____ 16. et   p. to hesitate, doubt
_____ 17. dōnum, -ī   q. to shout
_____ 18. dominus, -ī   r. gift, present
_____ 19. clāmō, -āre   s. friend
_____ 20. audeō, -ēre   t. mind, spirit, courage
_____ 21. amīcus, -ī   u. to terrify, scare
_____ 22. puer, -ī   v. boy

VOCABULARY: DERIVATIVES. Write the English word from the list below, derived from one of the Chapter 2 vocabulary words, that completes the following English sentences in the first blank, and write the Latin word from which it is derived in the second blank. The blank for the English word has been divided into individual blanks for each letter for assistance.

agriculture amicable animated belligerent
dominated locaton   puerile   virility
audacious   clamor

1. The _____ of the treasure was kept secret so no one could find it.

— — — — — — — —   _____

2. It was an _____ move; no one expected it.

— — — — — — — — —   _____

3. She is _____; she wants to get in a fight.

— — — — — — — — — — — _____

4. You need to be more _____; people think you're dead.

— — — — — — — —   _____

5. People like him because he's so _____; he gets along with everyone.

— — — — — — — —   _____

6. Stop acting so immature! You're being _____.

— — — — — — —   _____

7. The commotion caused quite a _____; no one could hear anything because of all of the noise.

— — — — — —   _____

8. His _____ is palpable; he wears his masculinity on his sleeve.

— — — — — — — —   _____

9. He wants to be a farmer; he's studying _____.

— — — — — — — — — — — _____

10. She _____ the competition; no one could touch her.

— — — — — — — — —   _____

CHAPTER **3**

SECTION 16: GENITIVE CASE. Below are word pairs of one nominative noun and one genitive noun. Circle the genitive and translate the word pairs. The vocabulary is from the Chapter 3 vocabulary list.

fābula <u>deōrum</u>   **the story of the gods**

1. deōrum templum   _____

2. imperium ventī   _____

3. arma turbae   _____

4. caelī deus   _____

5. imperium librōrum   _____

6. deōrum arma   _____

7. deus armōrum   _____

8. turbārum imperium   _____

9. caelī dī   _____

10. fābulārum imperium   _____

SECTION 16: GENITIVE CASE. Translate the English word pairs in brackets into Latin to complete the Latin sentence and translate the entire sentence into English below. One of the English words will be in the genitive and one will be in either the nominative or the accusative. Make certain to translate the non-genitive word into the correct case. The vocabulary comes from the first three chapters.

Agricola [fields of roses] amat.   **agrōs rosārum; The farmer loves fields of roses.**

1. Nauta [the nature of water] timet.   _____

_____

2. Virī [the plans of the master] dubitant.   _____

_____

3. [The spirit of the gods] virōs terret.   _____

_____

4. [The nature of the wind] nautās terret.   _____

_____

5. Puerī [stories of women] amant. _____

_____

6. Dominus [a temple of the gods] aedificat. _____

_____

7. Amīcus [the gift of books] dat. _____

_____

8. Fēminae [the story of the war] nārrant. _____

_____

9. [The gifts of the gods] virīs placent. _____

_____

10. [The stories of women] animum mōnstrant. _____

_____

SECTION 17: DATIVE CASE. Below are simple sentences, each of which contains a dative. Circle the dative and translate the sentence (if the dative is an indirect object, translate it both ways; refer to page 22 of your textbook if necessary).

Nauta fēminae rosam dat.　　　**The sailor gives the woman a rose.**
　　　　　　　　　　　　　　　　　The sailor gives a rose to the woman.

1. Ventus dīs nihil dat. _____

2. Fābula virīs imperium mōnstrat. _____

3. Dominī imperiō pugnant. _____

4. Nihil dominīs placet. _____

5. Amīcus puerīs puellīsque fabulās nārrat. _____

6. Vir fēminae dōnum dat. _____

7. Agricolae imperiō deōrum pārent. _____

8. Turba dominīs imperium mōnstrat. _____

9. Dī agricolīs fortūnam dant. _____

10. Nautae dīs fortūnam dēbent. _____

SECTION 18: EXPECTATIONS. Write the correct Latin word to complete the sentence in the blank to the right of the sentence, and briefly explain your choice in the blank below.

Deus _____ (templō, templum) aedificat.   templum

That deus is nominative and the verb is transitive would indicate a direct object which is accusative.

1. Amīcus _____ (deus, deōs) videt.   _____

_____

2. _____ (Ventus, Ventī) deō pārent.   _____

_____

3. Deus _____ (caelum, caelī, caelō) imperium mōnstrat. _____

_____

4. Vir fābulam _____ (turbae, turbam) nārrat.   _____

_____

5. Deus imperium _____ (turbae, turbam) mōnstrat.   _____

_____

6. Fābula imperium _____ (deus, deī, deō) mōnstrat.   _____

_____

7. Nēmō _____ (arma, armōrum, armīs) portat.   _____

_____

8. Turba arma _____ (deō, deum) mōnstrat.   _____

_____

SECTION 19: SENTENCE PATTERN: SPECIAL INTRANSITIVE. Choose the correct verb to complete the sentence based on the context that the rest of the sentence provides. Write your answer in the blank to the right of the sentence and translate the sentence in the space below.

Deus _____ templum (aedificat, audent).   **aedificat**
The god builds the temple.

1. Dominus librōs amīcīs (dat, pāret).   _____

_____

2. Dominus amīcīs (dat, pāret).   _____

_____

3. Deus templum (nocet, mōnstrat).   _____

_____

4. Deus templō (nocet, mōnstrat).   _____

_____

5. Ventus turbae (placet, pugnat).   _____

_____

6. Turba ventum (placet, pugnat).   _____

_____

7. Nēmō arma (portat, nocet).   _____

_____

8. Fābula dīs (nārrat, placet).   _____

_____

9. Dī imperium (mōnstrant, pārent).   _____

_____

10. Fābulae deō (nocent, nārrant).   _____

_____

VOCABULARY: DERIVATIVES. Write the English word from the list below, derived from one of the Chapter 3 vocabulary words, that completes the following English sentences in the first blank, and write the Latin word from which it is derived in the second blank. The blank for the English word has been divided into individual blanks for each letter for assistance.

armaments   celestial   deity   fabulous
imperious   nihilism   edifice   narrator
portable   pugnacious

1. _____ beings are invisible; they live in the heavens.

— — — — — — —   _____

2. The Parthenon is an imposing stone _____; it remains intimidating to even approach.

— — — — — —   _____

3. Mars' _____ attitude gets him into trouble; he's always looking for a fight.

— — — — — — — —   _____

4. Diana's _____ makes her difficult to work with; she doesn't want to follow any of the rules.

— — — — — — —   _____

5. How can we penetrate the defenses of the town? The _____ are just too strong.

— — — — — — — —   _____

6. Stop being so _____. You're not the one in charge.

— — — — — — — —   _____

7. That ballista is too big. We need one that is more_____.

— — — — — — —   _____

8. Not everyone requires a _____ to believe in; some people are just spiritual.

— — — — —   _____

9. What a _____ tale you tell! No one would believe it.

— — — — — — —   _____

10. Every story needs a good _____.

— — — — — — —   _____

CHAPTER 4

SECTION 20: THE ADVERB. In the English sentences below, circle the adverb, identify what it modifies, and identify what information it provides / what question it answers. Review p.27 in your textbook if necessary.

The man walks slowly.   **[adverb = slowly] modifies 'walks'; answers 'how the man walks'**

1. Marcus lives there. _____

2. The student really loves Latin. _____

3. Soon the guests will arrive at the symposium. _____

4. The chariot travels the course fast. _____

5. The ballista is too tall to fit through the gate. _____

6. The family walks together in the Subura. _____

7. Sadly the red team lost. _____

8. Today we will win the election. _____

9. The man walks too slowly. _____

10. The woman knows well what to do. _____

SECTION 21: ABLATIVE CASE. Change the number of the following ablative nouns.

    agrīs   **agrō**

1. casā _____   6. turbīs _____

2. pontīs _____   7. caelō _____

3. oculō _____   8. deō _____

4. fābulā _____   9. puerīs _____

5. librō _____   10. litterīs _____

SECTION 21: ABLATIVE CASE. As you learn more cases and case endings, endings will overlap more and more, e.g. –ō can be either the dative or the ablative. This overlap makes the use of context to determine case (rather than ending alone) increasingly important. Below are Latin sentences with an underlined noun whose ending is shared by another case. Identify the case of the underlined noun and explain how you made your decision. (Although the macron will distinguish 1st declension nominative and ablative singular, explain your determination using context rather than the macron alone; not every Latin text includes macrons.)

Vir prō f̲ē̲m̲i̲n̲ā̲ ambulat.   **ablative: object of a preposition that takes the ablative**

1. Fēmina v̲i̲r̲ō̲ dōnum dat. _____

2. Nauta prō a̲m̲ī̲c̲ō̲ nāvigat. _____

3. Amīcus o̲c̲u̲l̲ī̲s̲ viam videt. _____

4. Casae f̲ē̲m̲i̲n̲a̲e̲ placent. _____

5. Dī in c̲a̲e̲l̲ō̲ casam habent. _____

6. Puer ab a̲g̲r̲i̲c̲o̲l̲ā̲ festīnat. _____

7. Nēmō d̲o̲m̲i̲n̲ō̲ viam mōnstrat. _____

8. Fēmina puellae in c̲a̲s̲ā̲ fābulam nārrat. _____

9. Dominus d̲ī̲s̲ pāret. _____

10. Puerī ā v̲i̲ī̲s̲ errant. _____

SECTION 21: ABLATIVE CASE [ABLATIVE OF MEANS/INSTRUMENT]. These Latin sentences require an ablative of means/instrument to be complete. Translate the Latin and finish them with an ENGLISH ablative of means/instrument. Note that some sentences can be completed with different prepositional phrases (e.g. ones that answer the questions where? or when?); make certain that your prepositional phrase is an ablative of means. Refer to p.28 of Shelmerdine if necessary.

Vir _____ ambulat.   **The man walks *with/by means of a cane*.**

1. Puerī _____ virōs pugnant. _____

2. Virī _____ casam aedificant. _____

3. Puellae _____ librōs portant. _____

4. Dominus _____ amīcōs terret. _____

5. Agricolae _____ casās movent. _____

6. Dominī _____ rēgnum superant. _____

7. Dī _____ deōs pugnant. _____

8. Puellae _____ clāmant. _____

9. Agricolae _____ amīcōs vocant. _____

10. Fēminae _____ rosās tenent. _____

SECTION 22: THE PREPOSITION. Complete the diagram below with the correct Latin and English preposition from the list in Chapter 4 (p.32; prō is not included). Some Latin prepositions will be used more than once because of differences in their English meanings.

Latin Preposition   English Preposition   Latin Preposition   English Preposition

1. _____   _____   5. _____   _____

2. _____   _____   6. _____   _____

3. _____   _____   7. _____   _____

4. _____   _____   8. _____   _____

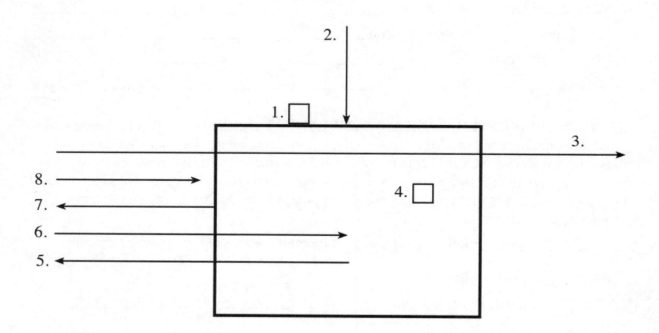

SECTION 23: EXPRESSIONS OF PLACE. Choose the correct Latin phrase to complete the following sentences and translate the sentences.

Dī ____ (ad caelum, in caelō, caelō) festīnant.   *ad caelum*
The gods hurry to the sky.

1. Nēmō ____ (ad pontum, pontō, ad pontō) ambulat. _____

_____

2. Dī ____ (ā casam, ā casā, casā) ambulant.   _____

_____

3. Amīcī ____ (in agrīs, agrīs, agrōs) errant.   _____

_____

4. Puerī ____ (ad pontum, nāvigāre, casae) festinant. _____

_____

5. Puellae ____ (in viīs, viā, viīs) festīnant.   _____

_____

6. Dominus ____ (bellō, ē bellō, bellum) movet.   _____

_____

7. Virī ____ (in pontum, pontō, in pontō) nāvigant. _____

_____

8. Agricolae ____ (in viam, in viā, viā) nēminem vident. _____

_____

9. Puellae ____ (ad amīcōs, amīcīs, amīcōs) dōnum dant. _____

_____

10. Nautae ____ (ad viam, viae, ad viā) aquam portant. _____

_____

VOCABULARY: DERIVATIVES. Write the English word from the list below, derived from one of the Chapter 4 vocabulary words, that completes the following English sentences in the first blank, and write the Latin word from which it is derived in the second blank. The blank for the English word has been divided into individual blanks for each letter for assistance.

casino   binoculars   antler   deviate   ambulation
errant   emotional   motor   navigable

1. The Romans gambled on horse races rather than in a _____.

— — — — —   _____

2. The Romans did not have _____ to see far away but they did have a form of eye glasses that helped correct their vision.

— — — — — — — — —   _____

3. Dido became very _____ when Aeneas told her that he was leaving her.

— — — — — — — —   _____

4. Unicorns don't have _____s like a deer but rather a single horn like a narwhal.

— — — — — —   _____

5. Relief sculptures show Roman cranes powered not by a _____ but by a slave in a treadwheel.

— — — — —   _____

6. The most common way for Roman soldiers to travel was _____; the only troop transports then were their feet.

— — — — — — — — —   _____

7. The Tiber looks slow and shallow but in ancient Rome it was perfectly _____.

— — — — — — — —   _____

8. Cupid's arrow at Apollo was not _____; it hit its mark perfectly.

— — — — — —   _____

9. Odysseus did not _____ from Athena's instructions when he returned home.

— — — — — — —   _____

CHAPTER 5

SECTION 25: THE ADJECTIVE. Identify the case, number, and gender of the following adjectives in the specified columns. For forms that have more than one possibility, more than one set of blanks has been included.

meus	nominative	singular	masculine
	case	number	gender
1. magnam	_____	_____	_____
2. multōs	_____	_____	_____
3. tuī	_____	_____	_____
	_____	_____	_____
	_____	_____	_____
4. aegrārum	_____	_____	_____
5. bonum	_____	_____	_____
	_____	_____	_____
	_____	_____	_____
6. malā	_____	_____	_____
7. lībrīs	_____	_____	_____
	_____	_____	_____
	_____	_____	_____
	_____	_____	_____
	_____	_____	_____
	_____	_____	_____
8. parvōrum	_____	_____	_____
	_____	_____	_____
9. dīvīnus	_____	_____	_____
10. altās	_____	_____	_____

SECTION 26: AGREEMENT. Choose the adjective that agrees with the noun at left.

terrās	altīs	**altās**	altae
1. silvī	pulcher	pulchrī	pulchrae
2. terrae	dīvīnus	dīvīna	dīvīnae
3. saxa	magnā	magnum	magna
4. oculōs	meus	meōs	meās
5. nēmō	parvō	parvī	parvus
6. agricola	altus	alta	altā
7. rosīs	pulchrī	pulchrīs	pulchrā
8. nautās	aegra	aegrās	aegrōs
9. nihil	bonō	bonī	bonum
10. sapientiārum	tuārum	tuae	tuā

SECTION 26: AGREEMENT. Form the adjective in parentheses to agree with the specified noun. Write both words for your answer.

saxō (magnus, -a, -um)   saxō magnō

1. sapientiae (noster, nostra, nostrum) _____

2. terrā (tuus, -a, -um) _____

3. saxa (parvus, -a, -um) _____

4. cūrārum (dīvīnus, -a, -um) _____

5. nautās (pulcher, pulchra, pulchrum) _____

6. ager (bonus, -a, -um) _____

7. agricolae (not dative; aeger, aegra, aegrum) _____

8. nēmō (līber, lībera, līberum) _____

9. dōnum (malus, -a, -um) _____

10. nautā (meus, -a, -um) _____

SECTION 26: AGREEMENT. Make each adjective agree with one of the nouns in the sentence and translate the sentence. It doesn't matter which adjective goes with which noun but you must translate the sentence with your noun – adjective pairs correct.

Vir saxum tenet. (magnus, -a, -um; parvus, -a, -um)
Vir *parvus* saxum *magnum* tenet. The small man holds a large rock.

1. Dominī cūrās habent. (malus, -a, -um; multus, -a, -um)

new Latin sentence with adjectives: _____

English translation of new sentence: _____

2. Turba dominō sapientiam mōnstrat. (meus, -a, -um; noster, -tra, -trum; tuus, -a, -um)

new Latin sentence with adjectives: _____

English translation of new sentence: _____

3. Via in terrā errat. (bonus, -a, -um; malus, -a, -um)

new Latin sentence with adjectives: _____

English translation of new sentence: _____

4. Dī ad caelum arma portant. (altus, -a, -um; multus, -a, -um; aeger, -gra, -grum)

new Latin sentence with adjectives: _____

English translation of new sentence: _____

5. Virī saxīs casās aedificant. (dīvīnus, -a, -um; altus, -a, -um, multus, -a, -um)

new Latin sentence with adjectives: _____

English translation of new sentence: _____

SECTION 28: SUM: PRESENT INDICATIVE AND INFINITIVE. Write the correct form of *sum* to correctly translate the underlined English.

They are cold.   **sunt**

1. We are tall.   _____

2. They are lovely.   _____

3. I am exhausted.   _____

4. You all are amazing.   _____

5. He is too loud.   _____

6. You (s.) are effervescent.   _____

7. She is an athlete.   _____

8. They are teachers.   _____

9. It is too dark in here.   _____

10. We are funny.   _____

SECTION 28: SUM: PRESENT INDICATIVE AND INFINITIVE. In English, 'to be' (Latin *sum*) can be used either as a main verb or as a helping verb. It is important to understand that Latin does not use *sum* as a helping verb (at least not for present stem tenses). In the blanks to the left of the sentences below, identify whether the underlined form of *sum* is a main verb (MV) or a helping verb (HV).

_HV_ The man is running home.

_____ 1. Amazons are very tall.

_____ 2. Are you seeing the gladiatorial combat?

_____ 3. We are watching too much Greek comedy.

_____ 4. You all are very barbaric.

_____ 5. I am so tired of Nero's antics.

_____ 6. They are driving their chariot too quickly.

_____ 7. She is winning the race.

_____ 8. Seneca's dramas are bombing.

_____ 9. You and I need to be more discerning in our political affiliations.

_____ 10. Icarus wants to be flying by now.

SECTION 30: MORE USES OF THE ABLATIVE. With the introduction of the ablatives of accompaniment and manner, in addition to the ablative of instrument / means, the English word 'with' takes on three very different uses. In the blanks to the left of the sentences below, identify whether the underlined prepositional phrase using 'with' is an ablative of instrument / means (IN), manner (MA), or accompaniment (AC).

_____ 1. The team won the race with a trick play.

_____ 2. Each parent went to the play with her child.

_____ 3. They were fighting with each other.

_____ 4. With great sadness Andromache watched her husband leave.

_____ 5. The student completed her assignment with a stylus.

_____ 6. They heard about the status of the battle with great surprise.

_____ 7. The Pompeian room was painted <u>with great care</u>.

_____ 8. The mime spoke <u>with his hands</u>.

_____ 9. The poet spoke <u>with his friend</u>.

_____ 10. The soldier spoke <u>with great pain</u>.

SECTION 30: MORE USES OF THE ABLATIVE. Choose the correct 'with' ablative to finish the Latin sentences below and translate the sentence.

Dominus (saxīs, cum saxīs) casam aedificat.
saxīs: The master builds his house with stones.

1. Fēmina (sapientiā, cum sapientiā) imperium habet.

_____   _____

2. Dī (armīs, cum armīs) virōs pugnant.

_____   _____

3. Vir (turbā, cum turbā) ambulat.

_____   _____

4. Nēmō (cūrā, cum cūrā) terret.

_____   _____

5. Puerī (puellīs, cum puellīs) docent.

_____   _____

6. Nautae (fortūnā, cum fortūnā) nāvigant.

_____   _____

7. Puella (animō, cum animō) amīcōs terret.

_____   _____

8. Dominī (cūrā, cum cūrā) agricolīs librum dant.

_____   _____

9. Puerī (rosīs, cum rosīs) puellās amant.

_____   _____

10. Dī (ventīs, cum ventīs) movent.

_____   _____

VOCABULARY: DERIVATIVES. Write the English word from the list below, derived from one of the Chapter 5 vocabulary words, that completes the following English sentences in the first blank, and write the Latin word from which it is derived in the second blank. The blank for the English word has been divided into individual blanks for each letter for assistance.

accurate	curiosity	sylvan	disinter
terrestrial	conjecture	future	altitude
bonbon	divinity	liberate	magnanimous
malaria	multiple	pulchritude	

1. Could we confirm the number of stab wounds if we _____red Caesar's body?

   — — — — — — —   _____

2. In general an augur had to see _____ birds in flight to determine the _____; one usually was not enough.

   — — — — — — — —   _____

   — — — — — —   _____

3. Diana was a _____ _____; she was a goddess who not only frequented the woods but lived a wild and untamed life.

   — — — — — —   _____

   — — — — — — — —   _____

4. Tarquinius was attracted to Lucretia's _____ and chastity but her rape caused the Romans to _____ themselves from the tyranny of their monarchy.

   — — — — — — — — — —   _____

   — — — — — — — —   _____

5. The disease _____ is commonly associated with Africa but the Romans suffered from it as well.

   — — — — — — —   _____

6. Psyche's _____ caused the end of her marriage; she had to see the face of her husband.

   — — — — — — — —   _____

7. Mt. Olympus is the largest mountain with respect to _____, which is why the Greeks believed that it was the home of the gods.

   — — — — — — — —   _____

8. Although the Romans had dessert, usually fruit, nuts, or cakes, they would not have eaten the delicate _____s that we often enjoy.

— — — — — —   _____

9. Debating whether Homer is one person or multiple is _____; there is no conclusive evidence to confirm either hypothesis.

— — — — — — — — —   _____

10. The gods could be _____, giving and rewarding freely, but if they were crossed, they could become angry very quicly.

— — — — — — — — —   _____

11. The census was instituted as a way to have an _____ count of citizens so that they could be properly taxed and enrolled in the military.

— — — — — —   _____

12. The gods often stayed out of the lives of mortals, but would sometimes make _____ visits to interact with mortals when necessary.

— — — — — — — — —   _____

CHAPTER 6

SECTION 31: IMPERFECT ACTIVE INDICATIVE (FIRST AND SECOND CONJUGATION).
Translate the following Latin verb forms in three different ways. (Although the imperfect is
the focus of this exercise, not all verbs will be imperfect.) Refer to p.46 of your textbook for
the translations of the imperfect and p.8 of your textbook for the translations of the present.

intrābant	they were entering; they began to enter; they used to enter

1. parābāmus _____ _____ _____
2. manēbat _____ _____ _____
3. nūntiābam _____ _____ _____
4. intrant _____ _____ _____
5. iactābātis _____ _____ _____
6. ambulābant _____ _____ _____
7. errat _____ _____ _____
8. manēbant _____ _____ _____
9. nūntiābāmus _____ _____ _____
10. parābat _____ _____ _____

SECTION 31: IMPERFECT ACTIVE INDICATIVE (FIRST AND SECOND CONJUGATION).
Choose the English translation for the Latin verb form at left.

manēbat	he, she, it stays	<u>he, she, it was staying</u>	he, she, it stayed
1. nūntiābās	you report	you are reporting	you used to report
2. intrābāmus	we were entering	we entered	we will enter
3. parābant	they began to prepare	they are preparing	they did prepare
4. nūntiābam	we were reporting	they were reporting	I was reporting
5. manent	he, she, it was staying	they are staying	I did stay
6. movēbat	he, she, it moved	he, she, it moves	he, she, it kept moving
7. festīnābātis	you all hurry	you all will hurry	you all were hurrying
8. errābāmus	we tried to wander	we wandered	we wander
9. nāvigābant	we were sailing	they were sailing	he, she, it was sailing
10. ambulō	I was walking	I will walk	I walk

SECTION 32: FUTURE ACTIVE INDICATIVE (FIRST AND SECOND CONJUGATION).
Complete the following future verb forms to match the English at left.

I will stay   **maneBO**

1. we will prepare   parā _____
2. they will announce   nuntiā _____
3. he, she, it will stay   manē _____
4. I will enter   intrā _____
5. you (s.) will stay   manē _____

6. you all will enter   intrā _____
7. I will stay   manē _____
8. they will report   nuntiā _____
9. we will enter   intrā _____
10. they will prepare   parā _____

SECTIONS 31-32: IMPERFECT AND FUTURE ACTIVE INDICATIVE (FIRST AND SECOND CONJUGATION). Choose the Latin verb form for the English at left.

I will stay	**manēbō**	**manēbam**	**maneō**
1. he, she, it will enter	intrābit	intrābimus	intrābunt
2. I used to announce	nūntiābam	nūntiābō	nūntiō
3. they will remain	manēbit	manēbant	manēbunt
4. we prepare	parābimus	parāmus	parābāmus
5. you all will wander	errābātis	errābitis	errātis
6. they were moving	movēbunt	movēbant	movent
7. I will walk	ambulō	ambulābam	ambulābō
8. you (s.) are sailing	nāvigās	nāvigābās	nāvigābis
9. we were walking	ambulābāmus	ambulābās	ambulābam
10. you (s.) were fighting	pugnābātis	pugnābās	pugnābam
11. they are building	aedificābant	aedificābunt	aedificant
12. we give	dabāmus	damus	dabimus
13. I will show	mōnstrābō	mōnstrābimus	mōnstrābam
14. he, she, it will tell	nārrat	nārrābat	nārrābit
15. you all will carry	portābitis	portābātis	portātis

SECTION 33: THE IMPERATIVE. Form the singular and plural imperatives of the following verbs and translate each form.

maneō, -ēre   **manē stay**   **manēte (you all) stay**

1. intrō, -āre   _____   _____

2. parō, -āre   _____   _____

3. nūntiō, -āre   _____   _____

4. ambulō, -āre   _____   _____

5. moveō, -ēre   _____   _____

6. nāvigō, -āre   _____   _____

7. clāmō, -āre   _____   _____

8. terreō, -ēre   _____   _____

9. videō, -ēre   _____   _____

10. labōrō, -āre   _____   _____

SECTION 34: VOCATIVE CASE. Write the singular and plural vocative forms of the following nouns.

cēna, -ae   **cēna**   **cēnae**

1. populus, -ī   _____   _____

2. vīta, -ae   _____   _____

3. Ītalia, -ae   _____   _____

4. fīlius, -ī   _____   _____

5. pontus, -ī   _____   _____

6. pecūnia, -ae   _____   _____

7. fīlia, -ae   _____   _____

8. amīcus, -ī   _____   _____

9. saxum, -ī   _____   _____

10. oculus, -ī   _____   _____

SECTION 34: VOCATIVE CASE. Choose the correct Latin noun from the choices below to complete the Latin sentences. Be prepared to explain your choice.

_____, intrā silvam!	Fīlius	**Fīlī**	Fīliō
1. _____ cenam parat.	Rēgīna	Rēgīnā	Rēgīnam
2. _____ ad viam movent.	Turba	Turbae	Turbam
3. _____, rēgīna intrat.	Fīliī	Fīlius	Fīlī
4. Populusne cēnam parat, _____?	amīcus	amīce	amīcī
5. Fīlia, agricolane _____ parat?	terra	terrae	terram
6. _____, rēgīna in silvā manet.	Dominī	Dominus	Dominō
7. _____ sapientiam dubitant, puellae.	Amīcus	Amīcī	Amīce
8. Fīlī, cenam _____.	parat	parā	parāte
9. Manēte cum rēgīnā, _____.	fīlia	fīliae	fīlie
10. Intrā, _____, silvam cum fīliīs.	puer	puere	puerī
11. Nātūra nova manēre dēbet, _____.	deus	deī	dī
12. Nūntiāte, _____, nostram cūram.	domine	dominī	dominus

VOCABULARY: DERIVATIVES. Write the English word from the list below, derived from one of the Chapter 6 vocabulary words, that completes the following English sentences in the first blank, and write the Latin word from which it is derived in the second blank. The blank for the English word has been divided into individual blanks for each letter for assistance.

filial	pecuniary	populace	vitality
manor	nuncio	preparatory	novel
innovation	renovate	sinecure	

1. The _____ appeared at the gate with a message for the king.

— — — — —   _____

2. He was mad at his father but his _____ loyalty prevented him from yelling.

— — — — —   _____

3. His _____ was the place he went to get away; he could stay there without disturbance.

— — — —   _____

4. Free food and games for the _____! They will love you.

— — — — — — —   _____

5. The _____ of the machine was its use of water; no one had seen that before.

__ __ __ __ __ __ __ __   _____

6. Despite her advanced age, her _____ shone through in her active lifestyle.

__ __ __ __ __ __ __   _____

7. Seeing an opera in a Roman theater was a _____ experience for him.

__ __ __ __ __   _____

8. His _____ difficulty prevented him from being able to afford a new chariot.

__ __ __ __ __ __ __ __   _____

9. His desire to _____ the old villa spurred him on to learn carpentry.

__ __ __ __ __ __ __   _____

10. After all of that education, he is wasting his time in a _____, a job without any real work.

__ __ __ __ __ __ __   _____

11. The _____ school required him to wear his finest toga every day.

__ __ __ __ __ __ __ __ __   _____

CHAPTER **7**

SECTION 35: THIRD DECLENSION NOUNS. Write the stems of the following nouns (most are 3rd declension nouns but not all are).

dux, ducis   **DUC-**

1. corpus, -oris_____   6. dux, -cis _____

2. mors, -rtis _____   7. pater, -tris _____

3. uxor, -ōris _____   8. īra, -ae _____

4. homō, -inis _____   9. nūmen, -inis_____

5. māter, -tris _____   10. rēx, -gis _____

SECTION 35a-b: THIRD DECLENSION, MASCULINE, FEMININE, AND NEUTER. Complete the following chart as best as possible from memory. When necessary, use the paradigms on pp.51-52 for reference.

	rēx, rēgis	ars, artis	corpus, -oris
		singular	
genitive			
ablative			
nominative			
accusative			
dative			
		plural	
dative			
accusative			
nominative			
ablative			
genitive			

SECTION 35a-b: THIRD DECLENSION, MASCULINE, FEMININE, AND NEUTER.
With the introduction of third declension endings, you are now faced with more endings
whose case is dependent on declension, e.g. the –a ending, if first declension, is nominative
singular, while if second or third declension is nominative or accusative plural. Complete
the following Venn Diagram by placing all the endings of all declensions in the appropriate
space:

- if only a first declension ending, in the upper left
- if only a second declension ending, in the upper right
- if only a third declension ending, in the center bottom
- if shared by 1st & 3rd, in the center left
- if shared by 1st and 2nd, in the center top
- if shared by 2nd and 3rd, in the center right
- if shared by all, in the center

A list of endings is included below to ensure that you remember them all.

-a	-ae	-am	-ā	-ārum	-īs
-ās	-us	-ī	-ō	-um	-ōrum
-ōs	-ibus	-is	-em	-e	-ēs
-ium	---- [no set form]				

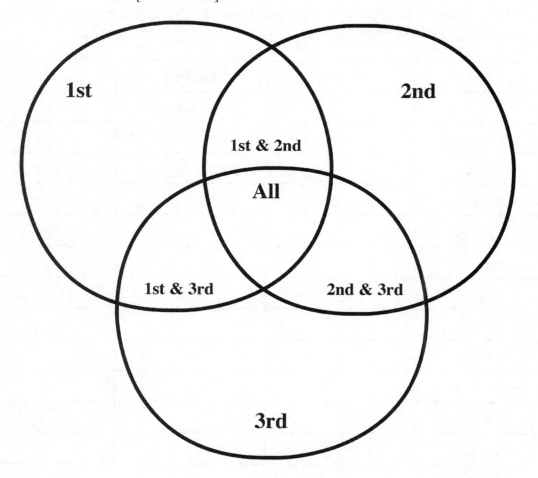

SECTION 35a-b: THIRD DECLENSION, MASCULINE, FEMININE, AND NEUTER. Identify the declension, case, and number of the following nouns (when there are multiple possibilities, include them all). Note that each noun will use an ending that is shared by more than one declension. It is imperative, then, to know the vocabulary information for the noun before answering.

capitī	3rd declension	dative case	singular number
1. frātrum	_____	_____	_____
2. fīlium	_____	_____	_____
3. saxī	_____	_____	_____
4. rēgī	_____	_____	_____
5. corpora	_____	_____	_____
6. īra	_____	_____	_____
7. exempla	_____	_____	_____
8. populī	_____	_____	_____
9. vīta	_____	_____	_____
10. artium	_____	_____	_____
11. hominī	_____	_____	_____
12. mātrum	_____	_____	_____
13. caelī	_____	_____	_____
14. templa	_____	_____	_____
15. ventum	_____	_____	_____

SECTION 35a-b: THIRD DECLENSION, MASCULINE, FEMININE, AND NEUTER. The increased overlap in endings among the three declensions now makes identifying noun – adjective agreement more difficult (no longer will agreement often be indicated by like ending). Choose the adjective that agrees with the noun at left.

artī	bonī	bonō	bonīs
1. civitās	nova	novās	novōs
2. īrā	dīvīnus	dīvīna	dīvīnā
3. homō	miser	miserī	miserō
4. mātrum	laetam	laetum	laetārum
5. corpus	meum	meus	mea
6. rēgis	magnus	magnīs	magnī
7. virtūs	parva	parvus	parvum
8. urbēs	pulchra	pulchrōs	pulchrās
9. nūminī	multīs	multō	multī
10. patrem	Rōmānus	Rōmānum	Rōmānōrum

SECTION 35a-b: THIRD DECLENSION, MASCULINE, FEMININE, AND NEUTER. The third declension, as you now know, has no set nominative form and no set gender. But there are some gender patterns that third declension nouns follow; these are listed on p.53 of your textbook. Use these patterns to identify the gender of the nouns (which are not part of your vocabulary) below.

piscātor, -ōris   **masculine**

1. vulnus, -eris	_____	6. lībertās, -ātis	_____
2. ratiō, -ōnis	_____	7. carmen, -inis	_____
3. aetās, -ātis	_____	8. genus, -eris	_____
4. scelus, -eris	_____	9. multitūdō, -inis	_____
5. imperātor, -ōris	_____	10. auctōritās, -ātis	_____

SECTION 36: IMPERFECT AND FUTURE OF SUM. Choose the correct English translation for the Latin at left.

erit	**he was**	**he is**	**he will be**
1. erant	they were	they are	they will be
2. sumus	we were	we are	we will be
3. erunt	they were	they are	they will be
4. erō	I was	I am	I will be
5. erat	he, she, it was	he, she it is	he, she, it will be
6. erimus	I will be	we will be	they will be
7. sunt	he, she, it is	they are	we are
8. erās	you (s.) were	I was	you (pl.) were
9. est	he, she, it was	he, she, it is	he, she, it will be
10. erit	he, she, it was	he, she, it is	he, she, it will be

SECTION 37: DATIVE OF POSSESSION. The dative of possession now introduces a third way to express possession in Latin in addition to the genitive (the most common) and possessive adjectives (e.g. meus, -a, -um; see the chapter 5 vocabulary list). In the Latin sentences below, identify in English who is doing the possessing and what method of possession is being used. Then translate the sentence.

Mēns laeta rēgī est.   **the king**   **dative of possession**
A happy mind is for the king /
The king has a happy mind.

	possessor	method of possession

1. Tua ars magna erit. _____ _____

_____

2. Mors ducī erit. _____ _____

_____

3. Vōx vēritātis regī sapientiam monstrat. _____ _____

_____

4. Cōnsul erat meus pater. _____ _____

_____

5. Propter bellum vēritās cōnsulibus erit. _____ _____

_____

6. Multum nūmen dīs dīvīnīs erat. _____ _____

_____

7. Manē in casā cum tuā cenā! _____ _____

_____

8. In bellō arma fēminīs virīsque erunt. _____ _____

_____

9. Misera mors bonīs et malīs erit. _____ _____

_____

10. Corpus cōnsulis in cīvitāte erat. _____ _____

_____

VOCABULARY: DERIVATIVES. Write the English word from the list below, derived from one of the Chapter 7 vocabulary words, that completes the following English sentences in the first blank, and write the Latin word from which it is derived in the second blank. The blank for the English word has been divided into individual blanks for each letter for assistance.

artifice	capitulate	consulate	corporation
corpulent	doge	fraternize	homage
irascible	maternal	numinous	patronage
regicide	urbane	uxorious	vociferous
lieutenant	commiserate		

1. Her _____ nature makes her difficult in the Senate House; everyone can hear her talking!

— — — — — — — — —   _____

2. Ovid's ____ tendencies made him stick out in the rural Tomis where he was exiled.

— — — — — —   _____

3. "I'm not sure my ____ is complete!" said Tullia as she backed up her chariot to run over the king again.

— — — — — — — —   _____

4. Uh oh: an ____ lion, something a gladiator never wants to see!

— — — — — — — —   _____

5. Augustus' wife Livia forced him to be _____; he could do nothing but pamper her.

— — — — — — — —   _____

6. Every general needs a good ____, someone who can have responsibility for lesser duties.

— — — — — — — — — —   _____

7. The wolf's ____ instincts must have taken over as she rescued the two young boys.

— — — — — — — —   _____

8. Marcus formed the Latium Plumbing ____ as a way to increase his business.

— — — — — — — — — — —   _____

9. Spartacus eventually had to _____; the might of Verres' army was just too great.

— — — — — — — — —   _____

10. Little Julius is without _____; what you see is what you get.

— — — — — — —   _____

11. Augustus paid _____ to his adopted uncle Julius by tracking down his killers.

— — — — — —   _____

12. You don't want to _____ with the Visigoths; you don't want your reputation to be damaged.

— — — — — — — — — _____

13. The palace of the _____ looks out over the Grand Canal; a fitting residence for a leader of the city.

— — — —   _____

14. Head to the _____ immediately; we must begin diplomatic negotiations before the Aedui cross the river.

— — — — — — —   _____

15. I can't fight anymore! I've become too _____ to enter the ring.

— — — — — — —   _____

16. The _____ countenance of Servius Tullius indicated that the gods had ordained him king.

— — — — — — —   _____

17. The Oscans and the Umbrians wanted to _____ about their conquest by the Romans.

— — — — — — — — — _____

18. No amount of _____ would protect Cicero from Antony's rage.

— — — — — — — —   _____

CHAPTER 8

SECTION 38: PERFECT ACTIVE INDICATIVE. Form both the present and the perfect stems of the verbs listed below.

doleō, dolēre, doluī	dolē-	dolu-
	present stem	perfect stem

1. parō, parāre, parāvī, parātus _____ _____

2. errō, errāre, errāvī, errātus _____ _____

3. moveō, movēre, mōvī, mōtus _____ _____

4. dō, dare, dedī, datus _____ _____

5. pugnō, pugnāre, pugnāvī, pugnātus _____ _____

7. ōrō, ōrāre, ōrāvī, ōrātus _____ _____

8. videō, vidēre, vīdī, vīsus _____ _____

9. iuvō, iuvāre, iūvī, iūtus _____ _____

10. vocō, vocāre, vocāvī, vocātus _____ _____

SECTION 38: PERFECT ACTIVE INDICATIVE. In the blanks to the left of each English sentence, identify whether the underlined verb is imperfect (I) or perfect (P). Review the difference between the two tenses on p.60 of your textbook.

P   The soldier <u>constructed</u> that night's defenses.

_____ 1. The senator <u>was running</u> to the Forum.

_____ 2. The miller <u>has ground</u> flour every day for the last two months.

_____ 3. Aeneas reluctantly <u>left</u> Dido for Italy.

_____ 4. Daphne <u>kept fleeing</u> Apollo.

_____ 5. The Romans <u>have</u> finally <u>conquered</u> Carthage!

_____ 6. Nero <u>rode</u> his horse into the Senate House.

_____ 7. Remus <u>has seen</u> six eagles.

_____ 8. Numitor <u>instituted</u> the census.

_____ 9. We <u>have been</u> to Rome five times.

_____ 10. That gladiator <u>has won</u> 52 times!

_____ 11. Rome <u>used to be</u> much smaller.

_____ 12. Hannibal <u>tried to conquer</u> Rome.

SECTION 38: PERFECT ACTIVE INDICATIVE. Complete the following verb forms with the correct ending to translate the English at left.

They grieved	**dolu-**	**ērunt**

1. We have walked.   ambulāv-   _____

2. They were hurrying.   festīnā-   _____

3. She has moved.   mōv-   _____

4. I built it.   aedificāv-   _____

5. She carried it.   portāv-   _____

6. We were showing them.   mōnstrā-   _____

7. They were fighting.   pugnā-   _____

8. They obeyed.   pāru-   _____

9. You all were shouting.   clāmā-   _____

10. Did you doubt?   dubitāv-   _____

SECTION 39: PERFECT ACTIVE INFINITIVE. Form the perfect active infinitive of the following verbs and translate the form.

narrō, -āre, -āvī, -ātus	**narrāvisse**	**to have told**
	perfect infinitive	translation

1. nāvigō, -āre, -āvī, -ātus   _____   _____

2. laudō, -āre, -āvī, -ātus   _____   _____

3. videō, -ēre, vīdī, vīsus   _____   _____

4. doleō, -ēre, -uī   _____   _____

5. teneō, -ēre, -uī, tentus   _____   _____

6. maneō, -ēre, mānsī   _____   _____

7. parō, -āre, -āvī, -ātus   _____   _____

8. nūntiō, -āre, -āvī, -ātus   _____   _____

9. iactō, -āre, -āvī, -ātus   _____   _____

10. moveō, -ēre, mōvī, mōtus   _____   _____

SECTION 40: FORMS OF POSSUM. Choose the correct translation for the Latin verb form at left. Note that forms of both *possum* and *sum* are included.

possumus	**we are**	**we are able**	**we were able**
1. poterunt	they are able	they were able	they will be able
2. potest	he, she, it is able	he, she, it was able	he, she, it will be able
3. sumus	we are	we were	we will be
4. poteramus	we are able	we were able	we will be able
5. possunt	we are able	they are	they are able
6. potestis	we are able	you (s.) are able	you all are able
7. est	he, she, it is able	he, she, it is	he, she, it was
8. es	we are	you (s.) are	they are
9. poterant	they are able	they were able	they will be able
10. possum	we are able	I am able	they are able

SECTION 41: INFINITIVE AS A NOUN. Identify in the blanks to the left whether the underlined infinitives are used as a noun (N) or as a complementary (C) infinitive; then translate the sentence. Be prepared to explain your answer. Review the uses of the infinitive on p.9 and on pp.61 and 62.

C	<u>Pugnāre</u> possumus.	We are able to fight.

_____ 1. Dolēre mortem bonum est. _____

_____ 2. Fēminīs rosās dare solēmus. _____

_____ 3. Habēre imperium rēgibus placet. _____

_____ 4. Laudāre deōs dīvīnum est. _____

_____ 5. Ambulāre saepe placet. _____

_____ 6. In Ītaliā diū manēre possunt. _____

_____ 7. Intrāre silvam puerōs terret. _____

_____ 8. Nāvigāre nautīs placet. _____

_____ 9. Dī hominibus sapientiam monstrāre optant. _____

_____ 10. Dare amīcīs pecūniam placet. _____

VOCABULARY: DERIVATIVES. Write the English word from the list below, derived from one of the Chapter 8 vocabulary words, that completes the following English sentences in the first blank, and write the Latin word from which it is derived in the second blank. The blank for the English word has been divided into individual blanks for each letter for assistance.

colleague   libertarian   lunacy   elucidate
amount   nominal   nominate   cooperate
tripartite   patriotic   pacify   perilous
rationale   verbose   dolorous   omnipotent
declaration   plenary   desecrate

1. We need to _____ a viable candidate; Rome needs a new bath complex.

— — — — — — —   _____

2. Her _____ seems to be spreading; she's wearing a white toga after Labor Day.

— — — — — —   _____

3. Uh oh: here comes Cicero. We know how _____ he can be. He never shuts up.

— — — — — — —   _____

4. We better get there early to get a seat; everyone will be at the _____ session.

— — — — — — —   _____

5. The Senate will have to _____ how this policy will work; right now it's unclear.

— — — — — — — — —   _____

6. Roman history has a _____ division: Monarchy, Republic, Empire.

— — — — — — — — — —   _____

7. Contrary to popular belief, the Roman gods are not _____; they can't do everything.

— — — — — — — — — —   _____

8. The heroes of the Monarchy and early Republic were _____; they sacrificed for their country.

— — — — — — — — —   _____

9. Ajax _____d the temple of Athena and was punished for it.

— — — — — — — — —   _____

10. The general surrounds himself with good _____s. They help him do his job.

— — — — — — — — —   _____

11. "Brutus, perhaps a _____ candidate is what we need. That way, we can do what we want."

— — — — — — — — —   _____

12. Pompey said to Caesar, "Why can't we just _____? We'd get more done that way."

— — — — — — — —   _____

13. That is a significant _____ of money for chariot repairs.

— — — — — —   _____

14. Theseus' return home as a young man was made _____ by his father's wife Medea who tried to kill him.

— — — — — — — —   _____

15. Such a _____ fee for extra votes in the praetorian election; what a bargain!

— — — — — —   _____

16. The Athenians tried to _____ the Persians but the damage had been done. Invasion was imminent.

— — — — — —   _____

17. What is your _____, Caesar, for building a forum next to the Roman Forum?

— — — — — — — —   _____

18. The Horatius family spent a _____ day after two of its sons and one of its daughters were killed.

— — — — — — —   _____

19. The Senate made a _____ that Marius could be consul more than once, something previously not allowed.

— — — — — — — — —   _____

CHAPTER 9

SECTION 42: THIRD CONJUGATION. Identify the conjugation of the following verbs in the blanks to the left with a 1, 2, 3, 3-iō.

3   dīscō, dīscere

_____ 1. valeō, valēre   _____ 6. capiō, capere

_____ 2. scrībō, scrībere   _____ 7. parō, parāre

_____ 3. ambulō, ambulāre   _____ 8. dīcō, dīcere

_____ 4. faciō, facere   _____ 9. mittō, mittere

_____ 5. agō, agere   _____ 10. sedeō, sedēre

SECTION 42: THIRD CONJUGATION. Choose the correct Latin form for the English at left.

He is writing.	**scrībat**	**scrībit**	**scrībet**
1. We are leading.	dūcimus	dūcit	dūcunt
2. They are ruling.	regunt	regit	regiunt
3. You (s.) are grieving.	dolet	dolēmus	dolēs
4. I am winning.	vincō	vincam	vincimus
5. I am capturing.	capiam	capiō	capimus
6. She is saying.	dīcet	dīcat	dīcit
7. They are doing it.	faciunt	fēcerunt	facit
8. You all are sitting.	sedētis	sēdisti	sedeātis
9. We are writing.	scrībāmus	scrībimus	scrībēmus
10. They are learning.	dīscant	dīscunt	dīscent
11. Speak (s.)!	dīcis	dīc	dīcite
12. to perform	age	agite	agere
13. He is capturing.	capit	capiunt	capere
14. Rule (pl.)!	regitis	rege	regite
15. Sit (s.)!	sedē	sedēs	sedētis
16. to do	facere	fac	facite
17. I am driving.	agō	agimus	agunt
18. They are conquering.	vincant	vincunt	vincent
19. Do it (s.)!	facite	fac	facere
20. Write (pl.)!	scrībite	scrībe	scrībere

SECTION 43: THE PRONOUN. Underline the English pronoun in the sentence below and identify its person and number.

The centurion terrified <u>us</u>.　　　　　**1st person　　plural**

　　　　　　　　　　　　　　　　　　　　　　person　　　　　　　　number

1. Did you all see the size of that ballista?　　_____　　_____

2. Do you want to come to the amphitheater?　　_____　　_____

3. Caesar said that we should meet him here.　　_____　　_____

4. I went to the baths but no one was there.　　_____　　_____

5 Brutus is accompanying you all to Delphi　　_____　　_____

6. The priests want us at the temple immediately.　　_____　　_____

7. Tell me what happened in the Senate House.　　_____　　_____

8. Give the wax tablets to us to respond.　　_____　　_____

9. I saw you alone standing outside Cicero's house.　　_____　　_____

10. We need more sestertii to buy this house.　　_____　　_____

SECTION 43: THE PRONOUN. Complete the following chart as best as possible from memory. When necessary, use the paradigms on p. 67 for reference.

	ego	tū
	singular	
genitive		
ablative		
nominative		
accusative		
dative		
	plural	
dative		
accusative		
nominative		
ablative		
genitive		

SECTION 43: THE PRONOUN. Change the number of the following pronoun forms. If there is one than one possibility, the one that it is not will be specified.

nōbīs (not abl.)   **mihi**

1. nōs (not acc.)   _____   6. vestrum   _____

2. tē (not abl.)   _____   7. meī   _____

3. vōs (not nom.)   _____   8. nōs (not nom.)   _____

4. ego   _____   9. tibi   _____

5. nostrum   _____   10. tū   _____

VOCABULARY: DERIVATIVES. Write the English word from the list below, derived from one of the Chapter 9 vocabulary words, that completes the following English sentences in the first blank, and write the Latin word from which it is derived in the second blank. The blank for the English word has been divided into individual blanks for each letter for assistance.

charming	agitation	coagulate	prodigious
caption	captivate	dictum	dictator
disciple	conducive	factious	compromise
missive	regulate	scribble	sedative
sedentary	convalescence	invincible	egocentric
interruption			

1. The tribune of the plebs is stirring up _____; the commoners are beginning to revolt.

— — — — — — — —   _____

2. What a _____ bulla you've made. It's perfect for an adolescent.

— — — — — — —   _____

3. The Gauls learned in the 4th c. BCE that Rome was not _____ when they breached the walls.

— — — — — — — — —   _____

4. The public baths are not _____ to relaxation; there are too many people around.

— — — — — — — —   _____

5. You want to _____ on the temple walls? That would be a desecration!

— — — — — — —   _____

6. Tiro was Cicero's slave but also his _____; he both helped and learned from Cicero.

— — — — — — —   _____

7. The provincial governor has become too _____. All he does is sit around his palace.

— — — — — — — —   _____

8. Pull the pilum out so that the blood can _____.

— — — — — — — —   _____

9. What is the _____ about? We cannot be disturbed.

— — — — — — — — — — —   _____

10. Hercules possessed _____ strength; he strangled two snakes when he was an infant.

— — — — — — — — —   _____

11. Pompey has been able to successfully _____ piracy in the Mediterranean; it not longer exists.

— — — — — — —   _____

12. The emperor has issued a _____ that mandates a rise in taxes.

— — — — — —   _____

13. The _____ of Aeneas after his wound was brief; he quickly returned to battle.

— — — — — — — — — — — —   _____

14. We need a _____ for this fresco; no one will know what it is without one.

— — — — — —   _____

15. Is Augustus _____? There are statues of him everywhere but does he need to bolster his rule?

— — — — — — — — —   _____

16. Augustus could have used a _____ to calm him down when he found out about the promiscuity of his daughter.

— — — — — — —   _____

17. By all accounts, Cleopatra was able to _____ men easily; they couldn't resist her.

— — — — — — — —   _____

18. The first speech of the _____ detailed how he consolidated governmental power.

— — — — — — —   _____

19. By its very nature, politics is _____; Roman politics was no different: everyone took sides.

— — — — — —   _____

20. _____ was not an option for Lucretia; she could not live with what happened to her.

— — — — — — — —   _____

21. Ovid sent numerous _____s to Rome from his exile in Tomis, hoping to be restored.

— — — — — — —   _____

CHAPTER **10**

SECTION 44: DEMONSTRATIVE PRONOUNS. Complete the following charts as best as possible from memory. When necessary, use the paradigms on pp.71-72 for reference.

	is	ea	id
		singular	
ablative			
nominative			
accusative			
dative			
genitive			
		plural	
accusative			
ablative			
dative			
genitive			
nominative			

	hic	haec	hoc
		singular	
genitive			
ablative			
nominative			
accusative			
dative			
		plural	
dative			
accusative			
nominative			
abaltive			
genitive			

	ille	illa	illud
		singular	
ablative			
nominative			
dative			
accusative			
genitive			
		plural	
genitive			
ablative			
nominative			
accusative			
dative			

SECTION 44: DEMONSTRATIVE PRONOUNS. Choose the correct demonstrative to agree with the noun at left.

lēgis	**illīus**	**illī**	**illīs**
1. montibus	huic	hīs	hī
2. perīculum	hōc	hunc	hoc
3. ratiōnī	illius	illī	illae
4. lūcem	illum	illam	illud
5. patriae	eius	ea	eō
6. poētā	eā	eō	eī
7. carmina	illō	haec	eā
8. nōmen	hunc	id	illum
9. verbō	illā	hoc	eī
10. mortem	hanc	eum	illud
11. homō	eō	illī	hic
12. corpus	ille	ea	hoc
13. frātrēs	illī	hīs	eius
14. patrum	hōrum	illud	eum
15. cīvitās	illōs	ea	hās
16. arte	haec	illā	eō
17. fīliō	eius	hōc	ille
18. cēnīs	illīus	eī	hīs
19. saxī	hūius	eō	illōrum
20. arma	eā	illī	haec

SECTION 44: DEMONSTRATIVE PRONOUNS. Make each demonstrative agree with the noun at left in the appropriate column.

partem	eam	hanc	illam
	is, ea, id	hic, haec, hoc	ille, illa, illud
1. pācem			
2. montī			
3. poētās			
4. verba			
5. carmine			
6. lēgēs (not. nom.)			
7. capitī			
8. fīliā			
9. factum			
10. caelō (not abl.)			
11. iūris			
12. nūminum			

SECTION 45: SPECIAL ADJECTIVES IN –ĪUS. Translate the following phrases into Latin, using the special adjectives listed on p.73 of your textbook. The case will be specified in parentheses when necessary.

the law alone (acc.)   lēgem sōlam

1. for the whole fatherland   _____

2. any reason (nom.)   _____

3. of another right / law   _____

4. with the whole part   _____

5. for one leader   _____

6. of any fathers   _____

7. with no voices   _____

8. for another poet   _____

9. of one poem   _____

10. any deed (acc.)   _____

VOCABULARY: DERIVATIVES. Write the English word from the list below, derived from one of the Chapter 10 vocabulary words, that completes the following English sentences in the first blank, and write the Latin word from which it is derived in the second blank. The blank for the English word has been divided into individual blanks for each letter for assistance.

factual	juror	cognoscenti	creation
centrifuge	subterfuge	incipient	adjudicate
legendary	lecture	persuasive	nullify
desolate	sullen	totality	unification

1. Can we use the _____ to isolate the element; it pushes everything else out from the middle.

— — — — — — — — — —   _____

2. Marius became a _____ politician because of his repeated reelection as consul

— — — — — — — —   _____

3. When Hercules heard about his twelve labors he became _____ and depressed.

— — — — — —   _____

4. Despite what Aristophanes says, Socrates _____d for free, teaching philosophy.

— — — — — — —   _____

5. The Romans conquered Carthage in _____, even sowing salt in the ground of the razed city.

— — — — — — — —   _____

6. Early Roman history is full of _____s, stories of dubious historicity whose purpose is to teach.

— — — — — — —   _____

7. The plain where Carthage once stood was _____ and barren after the Romans left.

— — — — — — — —   _____

8. Augustus and Maecenas assembled the best literary minds, the _____ of their day.

— — — — — — — — — — —   _____

9. Medea was very _____ with Creon; he allowed her to stay in Thebes one more day.

— — — — — — — — —   _____

10. Livy's history can be very _____ but his early history is less so, focusing on less reliable material.

— — — — — — —   _____

11. Tarpeia was punished for her _____; her underhanded betrayal of Rome cost her her life.

— — — — — — — — —   _____

12. The Roman _____ story involves a flood like the Judeo-Christian story.

— — — — — — —   _____

13. A panel of _____s _____d the fate of Orestes, determining in a court of law whether he was guilty of matricide.

— — — — —   _____

— — — — — — — —   _____

14. When Achilles spoke to Odysseus in the underworld, he tried to _____ his decision to die young and with glory.

— — — — — —   _____

15. _____ never occurred in Greece until Alexander created his empire.

— — — — — — — — — —   _____

CHAPTER 11

SECTION 48: FUTURE ACTIVE INDICATIVE (THIRD CONJUGATION). Identify the conjugation and the tense of the following verb forms.

relinquētis (relinquō, -ere)	**3rd conjugation**	**future**
	conjugation	tense
1. incipitis (incipiō, -ere)	_____	_____
2. persuādent (persuādeō, -ēre)	_____	_____
3. petēmus (petō, -ere)	_____	_____
4. crēdunt (crēdō, -ere)	_____	_____
5. sedent (sedeō, -ēre)	_____	_____
6. cadent (cadō, -ere)	_____	_____
7. legis (legō, -ere)	_____	_____
8. creat (creō, -āre)	_____	_____
9. cognōscēs (cognōscō, -ere)	_____	_____
10. fugiēs (fugiō, -ere)	_____	_____
11. capiētis (capiō, -ere)	_____	_____
12. scrībam (scrībō, -ere)	_____	_____
13. faciēmus (faciō, -ere)	_____	_____
14. dūcit (dūcō, -ere)	_____	_____
15. tenet (teneō, -ēre)	_____	_____

SECTION 48: FUTURE ACTIVE INDICATIVE (THIRD CONJUGATION). Change the number of the following verb forms.

cadēs   cadētis

1. relinquō	_____	6. crēdam	_____
2. petit	_____	7. iūdicās	_____
3. fugient	_____	8. incipiēmus	_____
4. creābit	_____	9. facient	_____
5. tenet	_____	10. legēmus	_____

SECTIONS 47-48: IMPERFECT AND FUTURE ACTIVE INDICATIVE (THIRD CONJUGATION). Form the present, imperfect, and future forms of the following verbs. The pronoun in parentheses will determine the subject. Then translate all forms.

vincō, -ere (nōs)	vincimus we conquer	vincēbāmus we were conquering	vincēmus we will conquer
	present	imperfect	future
1. crēdō, -ere (ego)			
2. relinquō, -ere (is)			
3. petō, -ere (vōs)			
4. iūdicō, -āre (nōs)			
5. fugiō, -ere (eī)			
6. faciō, -ere (tū)			
7. teneō, -ēre (eae)			
8. legō, -ere (ea)			
9. capiō, -ere (nōs)			
10. dīco, -ere (eae)			
11. mittō, -ere (is)			
12. scrībō, -ere (ego)			
13. sedeō, -ēre (nōs)			
14. agō, -ere (tū)			
15. parō, -āre (vōs)			

SECTIONS 47-48: IMPERFECT AND FUTURE ACTIVE INDICATIVE (THIRD CONJUGATION). Translate the underlined verb forms into Latin.

The centurion <u>was abandoning</u> his men.   **relinquēbat**

1. The Carthaginians <u>will flee</u> the Romans.   _____

2. Lucretia <u>used to believe</u> in the monarchy.   _____

3. Two Horatii and three Curiatii <u>will fall</u> in battle today.   _____

4. The Romans <u>will seize</u> Gabii through deception.   _____

5. Friends, you <u>will write</u> to Rome on my behalf.   _____

6. We <u>were learning</u> philosophy from Socrates himself.   _____

7. Brutus and the king's sons <u>were seeking</u> information.   _____

8. You <u>will read</u> for the next two hours.   _____

9. Marius <u>will lead</u> as consul nine times.   _____

10. I <u>will send</u> you a letter when I arrive.   _____

SECTION 49: NUMERALS. Complete the following problems in Latin using the cardinal numerals on p.84 of your textbook.

quattuor + ūnus =   **quīnque**

1. duodecim – decem =   _____

2. trēs + quīnque =   _____

3. sex – duo =   _____

4. novem + ūnus =   _____

5. trīgintā – vīgintī =   _____

6. ūndecim – quattuor =   _____

7. centum x decem =   _____

8. vīgintī – octō =   _____

9. sex + quīnque =   _____

10. octō – quīnque =   _____

SECTION 49: NUMERALS. Complete the following sentences with the correct Latin ordinal or cardinal numeral on p.84 of your textbook. Your Latin answer should reflect the appropriate case given the context.

George Washington was the _____ president.   **prīmus**

1. There were _____ kings of Rome.   _____

2. Romulus was the _____ king of Rome.   _____

3. Troy fell in the _____ year of the Trojan War.   _____

   [annus, -ī = year]

4. Odysseus was away from home for _____ years.   _____

   [annus, -ī = year]

5. There are _____ books of the *Aeneid*.   _____

6. Dido commits suicide in the _____ book of the *Aeneid*.   _____

7. Aeneas visits the Underworld in the _____ book of the *Aeneid*. _____

8. The Trojan Horse appears in the _____ book of the *Aeneid*. _____

9. There were _____ Punic Wars / wars with Carthage.   _____

10. The _____ Punic War occurred in the 2nd c. BCE.   _____

VOCABULARY: DERIVATIVES. Write the English word from the list below, derived from one of the Chapter 11 vocabulary words, that completes the following English sentences in the first blank, and write the Latin word from which it is derived in the second blank. The blank for the English word has been divided into individual blanks for each letter for assistance.

accusation	conjugal	flume	gratuity
congratulate	ingrate	lachrymose	laudable
militant	timorous	cascade	cadence
credence	incredulity	appetite	impetuous
petition	relinquish	dexterous	anterior

1. The client brought a _____ to his patron, hoping for decisive action.

   — — — — — — —   _____

2. A rousing _____ helped the legion fall into line.

   — — — — — —   _____

3. Actaeon was rightly _____ after he spied the goddess Diana bathing; she turned him into a stag.

   — — — — — — —   _____

4. Midas' golden touch betrayed his _____; he couldn't eat because all of his food turned to gold.

   — — — — — — —   _____

5. Tarquinius' sons reacted to the oracle with _____; they didn't believe what it said.

_ _ _ _ _ _ _ _ _ _   _____

6. Cicero leveled a scathing _____ at Cataline, detailing his conspiracy to assume power in Rome.

_ _ _ _ _ _ _ _ _   _____

7. Achilles _____ed his status within the army when he withdrew from the Trojan War.

_ _ _ _ _ _ _ _ _   _____

8. The _____ nature of Rome allowed it to control a vast empire.

_ _ _ _ _ _ _   _____

9. The _____ woman mourning her husband was Andromache.

_ _ _ _ _ _ _ _ _   _____

10. Jupiter could be a real _____ to his wife Juno; he never seemed to appreciate her.

_ _ _ _ _ _ _   _____

11. The Fons Bandusiae, not the largest waterfall, _____s in a peaceful flow over the rocks.

_ _ _ _ _ _   _____

12. Did the Romans use _____s to move their logs down the river?

_ _ _ _ _   _____

13. The Romans conducted business in the _____ of their homes; the back was private.

_ _ _ _ _ _ _   _____

14. Jupiter seemed to have _____ relations with everyone but his wife.

_ _ _ _ _ _ _   _____

15. The Romans use of engineering was _____; it allowed them both comforts and admirers.

_ _ _ _ _ _ _   _____

16. As a trusted orator and lawyer, Cicero commanded significant _____ when he spoke.

_ _ _ _ _ _ _ _   _____

17. Did the Romans leave a _____ for a meal well-prepared?

_ _ _ _ _ _ _   _____

18. Crassus begrudgingly _____ed Pompey on his political success.

_ _ _ _ _ _ _ _ _ _ _ _____

19. Nero was an _____ emperor; he acted rashly and without thinking.

_ _ _ _ _ _ _ _   _____

20. The ancient Cretans practiced a _____ sport that required them to hurdle moving bulls.

_ _ _ _ _ _ _ _   _____

CHAPTER **12**

SECTION 51: THIRD DECLENSION ADJECTIVES. Identify the declension of the following adjectives in the blanks to the left. If they are third declension adjectives, specify whether they are 1-ending, 2-ending, or 3-ending (see p.89 of your textbook to review these terms if necessary). Your answers then will be 2-1-2 or 3-1, 3-2, 3-3 (for 1-, 2-, or 3-ending third declension adjectives). None of the adjectives will be from current or previous vocabulary lists.

__3-2__   **mortālis, mortāle**

_____ 1. pār, paris

_____ 2. propinquus, -a, -um

_____ 3. similis, -e

_____ 4. dūrus, -a, -um

_____ 5. sapiēns, sapientis

_____ 6. gravis, -e

_____ 7. cārus, -a, -um

_____ 8. levis, -e

_____ 9. cūnctus, -a, -um

_____ 10. amīcus, -a, -um

_____ 11. fidēlis, -e

_____ 12. tristis, -e

_____ 13. īnfēlīx, īnfēlīcis

_____ 14. ūtilis, -e

_____ 15. paucī, -ae, -a

SECTION 51: THIRD DECLENSION ADJECTIVES. Form the following adjectives in the case, gender, and number specified.

brevis , -e: masculine, accusative, singular   **brevem**

1. omnis, omne: feminine, accusative, plural   _____

2. fortis, forte: neuter, genitive, plural   _____

3. ingēns, ingentis: neuter, nominative, singular   _____

4. ācer, ācris, ācre: masculine, ablative, singular   _____

5. difficilis, difficile: neuter, accusative, singular   _____

6. potēns, potentis: feminine, dative, singular   _____

7. dulcis, dulce: neuter, genitive, singular   _____

8. facilis, facile: feminine, ablative, singular   _____

9. fēlīx, fēlīcis: neuter, accusative, singular   _____

10. celer, celeris, celere: feminine, genitive, plural   _____

SECTION 51: THIRD DECLENSION ADJECTIVES. Make the adjective agree with the noun (not all adjectives will be third declension), rewriting the noun along with its adjective. When there is more than one possibility, more than one blank will be included.

fortis, -e: horā   **fortī horā**

1. omnis, omne: annī   _____   _____

2. fēlīx, fēlīcis: causam   _____

3. potēns, potentis: facta   _____

4. secundus, -a, -um: tempus   _____

5. dulcis, dulce: poētārum   _____

6. celer, celeris, celere: iūs   _____

7. facilis, facile: librō   _____

8. ingēns, ingentis: populōs   _____

9. brevis, -e: carmen   _____

10. difficilis, difficile: aetās   _____

SECTION 51: THIRD DECLENSION ADJECTIVES. Change the number of the following noun – adjective pairs. If there is more than one possibility, more than one blank will be included.

brevem hōram   **brevēs hōrās**

1. difficilēs lacrimae   _____

2. facilibus vītīs   _____   _____

3. ingēns pēs   _____

4. acris poētae   _____

5. fēlīcēs fīliī   _____

6. dulcia tempora   _____

7. potēns gēns   _____

8. omnī grātiā   _____

9. fortēs aetātēs   _____   _____

10. celeris flūminis   _____

SECTION 52: EXPRESSIONS OF TIME. In the following English sentences, underline the time expression and identify in the blank to the left of the sentence the time expression used: time when (TW), time within which (TH), length of time (LT).

__LT__   **Hannibal travelled through the Alps <u>for weeks</u>.**

_____ 1. Rome was founded in 753 BCE.

_____ 2. The Trojan War lasted for ten years.

_____ 3. There were three Punic Wars in the 3rd and 2nd centuries BCE.

_____ 4. Augustus officially became emperor in 27 BCE.

_____ 5. Ovid was exiled within a year of writing the Metamorphoses.

_____ 6. After the Julio-Claudian emperors, there was a year within which four men ruled.

_____ 7. Julius Caesar was killed on the Ides of March.

_____ 8. The Eastern Roman Empire fell in 1457.

_____ 9. Within one day three members of the Horatii were killed.

_____ 10. The Roman monarchy lasted for 244 years.

SECTION 52: EXPRESSIONS OF TIME. Choose the correct Latin phrase for the English time expression at left.

in this age	**in hāc aetāte**	<u>**hāc aetāte**</u>	**hanc aetātem**
1. for two hours	in duābus hōrīs	duābus hōrīs	duās hōrās
2. at that time	in illō tempore	illō tempore	illud tempus
3. for four years	in quattuor annōs	quattuor annōs	quattuor annīs
4. within three hours	tribus hōrīs	in tribus hōrīs	trēs hōrās
5. in nine moons	novem lūnīs	novem lūnās	in novem lūnīs
6. for her whole life	eius vītam omnem	in eius vītam omnem	eius vītā omnī
7. within twenty years	in vīgintī annōs	vīgintī annīs	vīgintī annōs
8. for one hour	ūnam hōram	ūnā hōrā	in ūnam hōram
9. in those years	illīs annīs	illōs annōs	in illīs annīs
10. within one moon	ūnā lūnā	ūnam lūnam	in ūnā lūnā

VOCABULARY: DERIVATIVES. Write the English word from the list below, derived from one of the Chapter 12 vocabulary words, that completes the following English sentences in the first blank, and write the Latin word from which it is derived in the second blank. The blank for the English word has been divided into individual blanks for each letter for assistance.

biennial	millennium (pl. = -a)	dolorous	gentrification
centipede	impede	contemporaneous	belligerent
indigestion	acrimonious	abbreviate	accelerate
celerity	dulcet	facility	felicitous
discomfort	omnivore	omnipotent	tertiary

1. The thought of eating dormice (a squirrel-sized rodent) like the Romans did gives me _____.

   — — — — — — — — — —   _____

2. The heroine Atalanta ran with great _____ but was tempted by the golden apples thrown to distract her.

   — — — — — — — —   _____

3. The Romans survived for over two _____ if you count the Eastern Roman Empire.

   — — — — — — — —   _____

4. Hector could not _____ fast enough to escape the marauding Achilles.

   — — — — — — — — — —   _____

5. The Roman Subura never underwent _____; it remained a neighborhood for the lower classes.

   — — — — — — — — — — — — — —   _____

6. The relationship between Crassus and Pompey was _____; they never got along.

   — — — — — — — — — —   _____

7. The Roman gods, despite what people think, are not _____; they cannot do anything.

   — — — — — — — — —   _____

8. The poet-hero Orpheus' lyre must have produced _____ tones to make the rocks weep.

   — — — — — —   _____

9. Not to be confused with biannual, _____ refers to something happening every two years.

   — — — — — — — —   _____

10. Big, tough Roman legionaries hate it when the creepy, crawly _____ invades their tents.

— — — — — — — — —   _____

11. Niobe wept _____ tears when Apollo and Diana killed all her children.

— — — — — — —   _____

12. Military leaders have a back-up plan, but do they have a _____ plan when the back-up fails?

— — — — — — —   _____

13. The god Vulcan, unlike the god of war Mars, is not at all _____; he prefers to create.

— — — — — — — — —   _____

14. Roman scribes tended to _____ frequently to save space on the page.

— — — — — — — —   _____

15. The Alps may have killed many of Hannibal's elephants, but it didn't _____ his march to Italy.

— — — — —   _____

16. Apollo had great _____ with the bow and arrow, but Cupid was even better with it.

— — — — — —   _____

17. The hydra has 100 heads but is it an _____? Will it eat anything with those heads?

— — — — — —   _____

18. The meeting of Odysseus and the Phaikians was _____ for him; they would eventually return him home.

— — — — — — — —   _____

19. _____ly to Rome's civil war and the fall of the Republic, some of the greatest works of Roman literature were produced.

— — — — — — — — — — — —   _____

20. To say that Prometheus spent his days in _____ is an understatement; an eagle ate his regenerating liver every day!

— — — — — — — —   _____

CHAPTER 13

SECTION 53: FOURTH CONJUGATION VERBS. Identify the conjugation of the following verb forms by writing its conjugation number in the blank to the left (do not forget about 3rd –iō verbs). Most verbs will not be familiar to you from your vocabulary lists.

__1__ cūrō, -āre

_____ 1. adveniō, advenīre

_____ 2. rapiō, rapere

_____ 3. trahō, trahere

_____ 4. vītō, vītāre

_____ 5. nesciō, nescīre

_____ 6. aperiō, aperīre

_____ 7. pōnō, pōnere

_____ 8. sentiō, sentīre

_____ 9. moneō, monēre

_____ 10. āmittō, āmittere

_____ 11. accipiō, accipere

_____ 12. cupiō, cupere

_____ 13. conveniō, convenīre

_____ 14. audiō, audīre

_____ 15. dormiō, dormīre

SECTION 53: FOURTH CONJUGATION VERBS. Choose the Latin verb form that translates the English at left.

he serves	servīt	<u>servit</u>	servet
1. we are sleeping	dormiēmus	dormīmus	dormiāmus
2. listen!	audīre	audīte	audī
3. they feel	sentiant	sentiunt	sentient
4. I understand	intellegō	intellegere	intellegam
5. you all know	sciētis	sciātis	scītis
6. he is hindering	impedit	impediet	impediat
7. to finish	fīnī	fīnīre	fīnīte
8. sleep (pl.)!	dormī	dormīte	dormire
9. they are listening	audient	audiunt	audiant
10. she feels	sentiunt	sentit	sentiet

SECTION 54: THE INTERROGATIVE PRONOUN. Complete the following charts as best as possible from memory. When necessary, use the paradigms on p.96 for reference.

	quis	quis	quid
		singular	
ablative			
nominative			
accusative			
dative			
genetive			
		plural	
accusative			
ablative			
dative			
genitive			
nominative			

SECTION 54: THE INTERROGATIVE PRONOUN. Choose the English translation for the Latin at left. Be prepared to explain your choice.

Quis dormit?   Who is sleeping?   For whom do you sleep?

1. Cūius cōpiae veniunt?   Whose troops are coming?   What troops are coming?

2. Quem senex audit?   Who hears the old man?   Whom does the old man hear?

3. Quō mīlēs cadit?   From what does the soldier fall?   Who kills the soldier?

4. Quid coniunx petit?   What does the spouse seek?   What seeks the spouse?

5. Quid cōpiam impedit?   What hinders wealth?   What does wealth hinder?

6. Cui senex cōpiam dat?   Whose old man gives wealth?   To whom does the old man give wealth?

7. Quid iter prohibit?   What does the journey prohibit?   What prohibits the journey?

8. Quem poēta legit?   Who reads the poet?   Whom does the poet read?

9. Quis mīlitī crēdit?   Who believes the soldier?   Whom does the solider believe?

10. Quem lēx relinquit?   Who abandons the law?   Whom does the law abandon?

SECTION 55: THE REFLEXIVE PRONOUN. Underline the pronoun in the following English sentences and identify it as Reflexive (R) or Personal (P). Then identify its case and translate it into Latin. When there is more than one answer, more than one set of blanks will be provided.

The girl hears <u>herself</u>.	**R**	**accusative**	**sē**
	r/p	case	Latin

1. The old man sees them. _____ _____ _____

2. Dido kills herself. _____ _____ _____

3. Brutus sees a leader in himself. _____ _____ _____

4. Augustus wants power for himself. _____ _____ _____

5. They see Nero fiddling. _____ _____ _____

6. Did you find yourself? _____ _____ _____

    _____ _____ _____

7. We see ourselves in the window. _____ _____ _____

    _____ _____ _____

8. The gladiators addressed us. _____ _____ _____

9. The Swiss Guard watched me. _____ _____ _____

10. I gave myself a gift. _____ _____ _____

    _____ _____ _____

11. The Horatii spoke among themselves. _____ _____

12. The Trojans criticized themselves. _____ _____ _____

SECTION 55: THE REFLEXIVE PRONOUN. Change the number of the following pronoun forms.

nōs   **ego**

1. sibi   _____   6. mē (acc.)   _____

2. vestrum   _____   7. suī   _____

3. ego   _____   8. sē   _____

4. tū   _____   9. nōbīs (dat.)   _____

5. vōbīs (abl.) _____   10. tibi   _____

SECTION 56: POSSESSIVE ADJECTIVES AND POSSESSION USING EIUS. Underline the possessive adjective in the following English sentences and identify it in the blank to the left as reflexive (R) or not (N).

___N___   **Our** favorite city was Rome.

_____ 1. The Greeks hid their soldiers.   _____ 6. Romulus killed his brother.

_____ 2. Priam talks about her people.   _____ 7. Scaevola burned his arm.

_____ 3. Clytemnestra kills her husband.   _____ 8. Patroclus uses his [Achilles'] armor.

_____ 4. Laocoon spears their horse.   _____ 9. Augustus exiles his daughter.

_____ 5. Daphne flees her suitor.   _____ 10. Zeus fears her wrath.

VOCABULARY: DERIVATIVES. Write the English word from the list below, derived from one of the Chapter 13 vocabulary words, that completes the following English sentences in the first blank, and write the Latin word from which it is derived in the second blank. The blank for the English word has been divided into individual blanks for each letter for assistance.

cornucopia	finial	itinerary	demur
senator	audience	dormant	impediment
intelligence	prohibitive	science	omniscient
sentient	servitude	venture	souvenir
dignity	immortality	paucity	reliquary
sapient	superiority	suicide	

1. I took a picture with a gladiator-reenactor as a _____ of my trip to Rome.

— — — — — — —   _____

2. The _____s met late at night to discuss the crisis facing the government.

— — — — — —   _____

3. Augustus met his _____ with great fanfare; he wanted them to enjoy their time before him.

— — — — — — —   _____

4. Odysseus rejected Calypso's offer of _____; he would rather die but experience life.

— — — — — — — — — —   _____

5. The symbol of the goddess Ceres is the _____; it overflows with the abundance of her harvest.

— — — — — — — — —   _____

6. The cost of Carrara marble makes it _____ for anyone but the aristocracy to use.

— — — — — — — — —   _____

7. The top of Augustus' mausoleum was crowned with a _____, a decorative element to finish it off.

— — — — — —   _____

8. Pygmalion had no idea that his statue would come to life, becoming a _____ being.

— — — — — — — —   _____

9. The plot to assassinate Caesar lay _____ until the time was right to strike.

— — — — — — —   _____

10. Odysseus' unplanned _____ took him throughout the Mediterranean on his long journey home.

— — — — — — — —   _____

11. Priam approached Achilles with _____ if with sorrow to retrieve his dead son's body.

— — — — — — —   _____

12. What is that finger-shaped container? It's a _____, something that contains the remains of a saint.

— — — — — — — —   _____

13. Ganymede _____red; he wasn't accustomed to having the king of the gods flatter him so.

— — — —   _____

14. Marius' low birth was an _____ to his upward mobility; he had to convince the aristocracy that they needed him.

— — — — — — — — —   _____

15. The gods are not _____; they don't know everything that happens.

— — — — — — — — —   _____

16. The Persians attempted to gather _____ about the Spartans to understand their enemy.

— — — — — — — — — — —   _____

17. The ancients were very interested in _____, though they approached knowing things from a more philosophical standpoint.

— — — — — —   _____

18. The Roman matron Lucretia committed _____ because she didn't want to live dishonored.

— — — — — —   _____

19. There is a _____ of writing from early Rome; its literature didn't begin until the 3rd century.

— — — — — —   _____

20. The Spartans proved their _____ over the Persians by fighting bravely even though they lost.

— — — — — — — — —   _____

21. Although Tiro lived his life in _____, Cicero in many ways treated him as a peer.

— — — — — — — —   _____

22. The _____ Alexander solved the riddle of the Gordian Knot.

— — — — — —   _____

23. The farthest north the Romans _____d was northern England; they did not conquer the Picts.

— — — — — — —   _____

CHAPTER **14**

SECTION 59: FUTURE ACTIVE INDICATIVE (FOURTH CONJUGATION). Identify the following verb forms in the blank to the left as either present (P) or future (F).

__F__ adveniet

_____ 1. intellegēmus	_____ 4. sciētis	_____ 7. prohibent
_____ 2. rapimus	_____ 5. veniunt	_____ 8. advenient
_____ 3. inveniēs	_____ 6. dīmittit	_____ 9. impediēmus

SECTION 59: FUTURE ACTIVE INDICATIVE (FOURTH CONJUGATION). Choose the correct translation for the Latin verb form at left.

monemus	**we are warning**	**we will warn**
1. rapient	they will seize	they are seizing
2. dīmittimus	we will send away	we are sending away
3. scītis	you all will know	you all do know
4. adveniēs	you will arrive	you are arriving
5. prohibet	she will prohibit	she prohibits
6. sentiēmus	we will feel	we are feeling
7. veniam	I will come	I am coming
8. intellegent	they will understand	they do understand
9. impediunt	they will hinder	they are hindering
10. audītis	you all will hear	you all do hear

SECTION 59: FUTURE ACTIVE INDICATIVE (FOURTH CONJUGATION). Complete the Latin verb forms with the correct endings of the future for the specified person and number, and then translate the forms. All verbs will be from either chapter 13 or 14.

2nd singular: dorm-	**-iēs**	**you will sleep**
1. 1st plural: aud-	_____	_____
2. 1st singular: sc-	_____	_____
3. 3rd plural: st-	_____	_____
4. 2nd plural: inven-	_____	_____
5. 3rd singular: mon-	_____	_____
6. 1st singular: cūr-	_____	_____
7. 3rd singular: rap-	_____	_____
8. 3rd plural: intelleg-	_____	_____
9. 3rd plural: prohib-	_____	_____
10. 2nd singular: imped-	_____	_____

VOCABULARY: DERIVATIVES. Write the English word from the list below, derived from one of the Chapter 14 vocabulary words, that completes the following English sentences in the first blank, and write the Latin word from which it is derived in the second blank. The blank for the English word has been divided into individual blanks for each letter for assistance.

arboretum	generic	honorary	hostility
legate	marinate	equinox	adventure
manicure	dismiss	invention	premonition
summon	rapacious	elongate	Mediterranean
tantamount	circumstance	circumnavigate	

1. Caesar had a _____ that he was going to die; he knew before it happened.

— — — — — — — — — —   _____

2. The 3-headed guard dog Cerberus had a _____ appetite; he would consume anything.

— — — — — — — — —   _____

3. The _____ was like a water-superhighway; it connected all of the cultures that bordered it.

— — — — — — — — — — — —   _____

4. Caesar's crossing of the Rubicon was _____ to declaring war on Rome.

— — — — — — — — —   _____

5. During the Empire, the title 'senator' became largely _____; it no longer meant anything.

— — — — — — —   _____

6. Jason's trip to the Black Sea was a journey of wonder and _____.

— — — — — — — — —   _____

7. The Romans sent _____s to the Parthians to recover their lost standard.

— — — — — —   _____

8. Caesar built a private forum that was then innovative but became _____ as others did too.

— — — — — — —   _____

9. The Romans had cosmetics; I wonder if they took care of their hands with _____s.

— — — — — — — —   _____

10. Marcus was hoping to _____ his dormice to give them more flavor.

— — — — — — —   _____

11. Seneca was _____ed by Nero, never a good thing; he reluctantly went to see him.

— — — — —   _____

12. Ovid was _____ed from Rome after Augustus became angry with him.

— — — — — —   _____

13. The _____ of waterproof concrete allowed the Romans to build in places others couldn't.

— — — — — — —   _____

14. The _____ of the Romans toward the Carthaginians was clear when they razed their city.

— — — — — — —   _____

15. The _____s under which Augustus assumed power were very complex.

— — — — — — — — —   _____

16. When Flavia wants to relax, she visits the _____; all the trees put her at ease.

— — — — — — —   _____

17. The _____ is when day and night are roughly the same length.

— — — — — —   _____

18. Aeneas _____d the eastern Mediterranean on his way to Italy from Troy.

— — — — — — — — — —   _____

19. Pinocchio's nose _____s when he tells a lie.

— — — — — — —   _____

CHAPTER 15

SECTION 61: PERFECT ACTIVE INDICATIVE. Identify the tense of the following verb forms and translate them.

cessit	perfect	he, she, it yielded
1. pōnit	_____	_____
2. cūrāvistī	_____	_____
3. invēnērunt	_____	_____
4. volvit	_____	_____
5. rapuimus	_____	_____
6. advenīmus	_____	_____
7. fīnīvī	_____	_____
8. sēnsistis	_____	_____
9. impedivēre	_____	_____
10. veniunt	_____	_____

SECTION 62: PLUPERFECT ACTIVE INDICATIVE. Choose the correct translation for the verb forms at left.

surrēxeram	I was getting up	I got up	<u>I had gotten up</u>
1. volvērunt	they rolled	they were rolling	they had rolled
2. rapuerant	they seized	they were seizing	they had seized
3. erāmus	we were	we are	we had been
4. advēneram	I arrived	I was arriving	I had arrived
5. āfuerās	you were absent	you are absent	you had been absent
6. temptāverātis	you all tried	you all are trying	you all had tried
7. erat	he was	he is	he had been
8. fuerat	she was	she is	she had been
9. posueram	I did put	I was putting	I had put
10. āfuerant	they were absent	they are absent	they had been absent

SECTION 62: PLUPERFECT ACTIVE INDICATIVE. Form the imperfect, perfect, and pluperfect of the verbs at left (the subject is specified by the pronoun in parentheses) and translate each of the forms.

fīniō, -īre (vōs)	fīniēbātis you were ending	fīnīvistis you ended	fīnīverātis you had ended
1. temptō, -āre (is)			
2. pōnō, -ere (nōs)			
3. adveniō, -īre (ea)			
4. moneō, -ēre (ego)			
5. rapiō, -ere (tū)			
6. cūrō, -āre (eī)			
7. stō, stāre (is)			
8. absum, abesse (ea)			
9. prohibeō, -ēre (eae)			
10. audiō, -īre (nōs)			

SECTION 64: PERFECT ACTIVE INFINITIVE. Identify the following infinitive forms as present (PR) or perfect (PF) in the blanks to the left of the verbs.

PF   **intellēxisse**

_____ 1. posuisse   _____ 5. surrēxisse   _____ 9. monēre

_____ 2. advenīre   _____ 6. stāre   _____ 10. temptāvisse

_____ 3. dīmīsisse   _____ 7. volvisse   _____ 11. scīvisse

_____ 4. rapuisse   _____ 8. cūrāvisse   _____ 12. abesse

VOCABULARY: DERIVATIVES. Write the English word from the list below, derived from one of the Chapter 15 vocabulary words, that completes the following English sentences in the first blank, and write the Latin word from which it is derived in the second blank. The blank for the English word has been divided into individual blanks for each letter for assistance.

aureole	civil	igneous	laboratory
litoral	limn	expectorate	provincial
undulate	cede	cessation	postpone
resurrection	tentacle	vault	durable
fortuitous	soprano		

1. An aqueduct cannot _____ over the countryside; it must remain straight to keep the water flowing.

   — — — — — — —   _____

2. Marcus and Lucius admired the _____ birds as they sat on the beach.

   — — — — — — —   _____

3. The Orpheus myth, when he returns from the underworld, can be read as a myth of _____.

   — — — — — — — — — — — —   _____

4. The prospect of the massive _____s of the terrifying sea monster kept the sailors out of the sea.

   — — — — — — —   _____

5. Venus and Juno were pretending to be _____ to one another when they really detested each other.

   — — — — —   _____

6. The Coliseum certainly is _____; it has lasted almost two millennia.

   — — — — — —   _____

7. The _____ nature of the Black Sea town Tomis didn't suit Ovid's urbane life.

   — — — — — — — — —   _____

8. Unfortunately, there was no denying Vesuvius' _____ nature in 79 CE when it erupted.

   — — — — — —   _____

9. The young Servius' head was not surrounded by the glow of an _____ but did have a flame dancing above it to signify his divine favor.

   — — — — — —   _____

10. To _____ during a gladiatorial match might be acceptable but never in front of the emperor.

   — —— — — — — —— — ——   _____

11. Nero prided himself as a singer; I wonder if he could hit the high notes of a _____.

   — —— — — — ——   _____

12. Jupiter _____d to Juno certain concessions so that she would stop harassing Aeneas.

   — —— — —   _____

13. Pliny the Elder was a scientist but much of his _____ was nature herself.

   — —— — — — — —— — ——   _____

14. The death of Laocoon was _____ for the Greeks because it eliminated any doubts about the Trojan Horse.

   — —— — — — — —— — ——   _____

15. Hadrian did not want to _____ the consecration of the Pantheon so he used 40 ft. columns instead of 50 ft. columns to keep it on schedule.

   — —— — — — — ——   _____

16. The Second Punic War brought a _____ of hostility between Rome and Carthage; Rome had defeated Carthage.

   — —— — — — — —— — ——   _____

17. I wonder if Pygmalion _____ed his statue before sculpting it or if he just began to sculpt without any preparatory drawings.

   — —— — —   _____

18. Some people think that the Temple of Juno Moneta was really a large _____ where Rome's money could be stored securely.

   — —— — — —   _____

CHAPTER 16

SECTIONS 65-66. FOURTH AND FIFTH DECLENSION NOUNS. Complete the following charts as best as possible from memory. When necessary, use the paradigms on pp.115-116 for reference.

	metus, -ūs	genū, genūs	fidēs, fideī
		singular	
ablative			
nominative			
accusative			
dative			
genitive			
		plural	
accusative			
ablative			
dative			
genitive			
nominative			

SECTIONS 65-66. FOURTH AND FIFTH DECLENSION NOUNS. Change the number of the following fourth and fifth declension nouns. When there is more than one possibility, more than one blank will be provided.

fluctuum   **fluctūs**

1. metus   _____

2. fīdem   _____

3. cornibus   _____

4. casūs   _____

          _____

5. faciēs   _____

          _____

6. genua   _____

7. fīdēbus   _____

          _____

8. fīdeī   _____

          _____

9. passum   _____

10. manuum   _____

SECTIONS 65-66. FOURTH AND FIFTH DECLENSION NOUNS. Make the specified noun agree with the adjective. When there is more than one possibility, more than one blank will be provided.

aureum: impetus, -ūs   **impetum**

1. longōrum: senātus, -ūs _____   7. superōs: metus, -ūs _____

2. mediā: spēs, speī   _____   8. fessō: cāsus, -ūs   _____

3. dīgnīs: rēs, reī   _____   _____

4. fēlīcī: cornū, -ūs   _____   9. tristēs: domus, -ūs _____

5. dulce: genū, genūs _____   10. aurea: genū, -ūs   _____

6. ūnius: diēs, diēī   _____

SECTIONS 65-66. FOURTH AND FIFTH DECLENSION NOUNS. Choose the correct Latin noun to finish the sentence from the choices in parentheses and translate each sentence.

Legatus nocte cum _____ (metus, metuī, _metū_) advenit.
The legate arrives at night with fear / fearfully.

1. Hostēs _____ (domus, domūs, domuum) cīvis rapuērunt. _____

_____

2. _____ (Fluctus, Fluctum, Fluctū) in lītus surrēxit.   _____

_____

3. Legatus _____ (faciēs, faciēī, faciērum) hostium petīvit. _____

_____

4. Alius cīvis cīvī aliī _____ (fīdeī, fīdem, fīdēbus) dedit.   _____

_____

5. Mater in puerī _____ (vultūs, vultuī, vultū) lūmen vīdit.   _____

_____

6. Servus ā _____ (genū, genūs, genua) surrēxit.   _____

_____

7. _____ (Cornū, Cornūs, Cornibus) _____ (impetus, impetuī, impetum) fēcit. _____

_____

8. Deus _____ (manuī, manum, manibus) arborem rapuit.   _____

_____

9. Hostēs in oculīs _____ (metus, metum, metū) vīdērunt.   _____

_____

10. Cīvis _____ (rēs pūblica; reī pūblicae; rem pūblicam) sērvīvit. _____

_____

SECTION 67: LOCATIVE. Identify in the blank to the left of the English phrases below whether or not those phrases in Latin would use a preposition (P) or not (N).

__P__ to the shore

_____ 1. to Rome

_____ 2. from the Mediterranean

_____ 3. in the country

_____ 4. to Carthage

_____ 5. from home

_____ 6. in Italy

_____ 7. in Athens

_____ 8. on the ground

_____ 9. from Africa

_____ 10. in Gaul

SECTION 67: LOCATIVE. Choose the correct Latin to translate the underlined English.

Vergil died in Brundisium.	**Brundisiī**	**Brundisiō**	**in Brundisiō**
1. Aeneas arrived in Carthage.	Carthāgine	in Carthāgine	Carthāgo
2. Aeneas left from Africa.	Africā	ab Africā	Africae
3. Aeneas sailed to Italy.	Ītaliam	Ītaliā	ad Ītaliam
4. Cincinnatus wanted to stay home.	domō	domī	domum
5. Cicero traveled to Athens.	ad Athēnās	Athēnās	Athēnīs
6. Horace had a villa in the country.	rūre	rūrī	in rūre
7. Caesar fought in Gaul.	in Galliā	Galliā	Galliae
8. Hannibal arrived from Spain.	Hispāniā	ab Hispāniā	Hispāniae
9. Augustus lives in Rome.	Rōmā	Rōmae	in Rōmā
10. Athens lies to the east of Rome.	Athēnae	Athēnīs	Athēnās

VOCABULARY: DERIVATIVES. Write the English word from the list below, derived from one of the Chapter 16 vocabulary words, that completes the following English sentences in the first blank, and write the Latin word from which it is derived in the second blank. The blank for the English word has been divided into individual blanks for each letter for assistance.

cornea	unicorn	meridian	domestic
fidelity	fluctuate	genuflect	impetus
manuscript	manufacture	meticulous	trespass
republic	rural	despair	ardent

1. Jupiter's _____ was always in question; he was not faithful to his wife Juno.

— — — — — — —   _____

2. Before the printing press, people read _____s, books written by hand.

— — — — — — — —   _____

3. Catullus felt _____ passion for his love Lesbia.

—— —— —— —— ——   _____

4. It is common to _____ before royalty as a sign of a respect.

—— —— —— —— —— —— ——   _____

5. What was Augustus' _____ for exiling Ovid? Why did he do it?

—— —— —— —— —— ——   _____

6. To write poetry in ancient meter requires a _____ attention to detail to get everything right.

—— —— —— —— —— —— —— ——   _____

7. Pegasus was a winged horse but was not a _____; he had no horns.

—— —— —— —— —— ——   _____

8. Horace enjoyed the _____ life as a way to escape the commotion of the city.

—— —— —— ——   _____

9. The sun is hottest at the _____ hour, when it is directly over top.

—— —— —— —— —— ——   _____

10. Ancient men had few _____ duties; their domain was outside of the home.

—— —— —— —— —— ——   _____

11. Under magnification, the _____ protrudes slightly from your eye.

—— —— —— ——   _____

12. The heroes of the _____ were distinguished by their self-sacrifice and dedication to the state.

—— —— —— —— —— ——   _____

13. Readers' opinions of Ovid have _____d over the years; some find him amusing and witty while some find him irreverent and unimportant.

—— —— —— —— —— —— ——   _____

14. Despite the decorated amphorae in museums, they were mass-_____d for storage and transport.

—— —— —— —— —— —— —— ——   _____

15. Romulus killed Remus for _____ing on sacred ground.

—— —— —— —— —— ——   _____

16. Agamemnon _____ed at the thought of sacrificing his daughter for favorable winds.

—— —— —— —— —— ——   _____

SECTIONS 69-71. PRESENT, IMPERFECT, FUTURE PASSIVE INDICATIVE. Identify the tense and voice of the following verb forms and translate them.

volvitur	present	passive	he, she, it is turned
	tense	voice	translation
1. spectāmus			
2. trahētur			
3. āmittēbāmur			
4. incenduntur			
5. currēs			
6. temptāberis			
7. cernēbantur			
8. pōnitur			
9. surgor			
10. cēdet			
11. adveniētis			
12. cūrābant			
13. audīar			
14. scīmus			
15. intellegeris			
16. gerēris			
17. crēdunt			
18. relinquō			
19. sentiētur			
20. prohibēbimur			

SECTIONS 69-71. PRESENT, IMPERFECT, FUTURE PASSIVE INDICATIVE. Change the number of the following verb forms.

surgis   **surgitis**

1. incendētur	_____	6. temptābiminī	_____
2. advenītur	_____	7. spectābāmur	_____
3. ardēbimur	_____	8. trahentur	_____
4. vidēbitur	_____	9. cernar	_____
5. rapiēmini	_____	10. inveniēmur	_____

SECTIONS 69-71. PRESENT, IMPERFECT, FUTURE PASSIVE INDICATIVE. Choose the correct Latin for the English at left.

it is burned	**incendētur**	<u>**incenditur**</u>	**incendit**
1. they will be dragged	trahuntur	trahētur	trahentur
2. I am established	īnstituor	īnstituar	īnstituō
3. you will be watched	spectābāris	spectāberis	spectēris
4. we were being seen	cernēbāmur	cernēbantur	cernēbar
5. they will be lost	āmittuntur	āmittentur	āmittantur
6. they are running	curruntur	currentur	currunt
7. she seems	videt	vidētur	videntur
8. it will be decided	cōnstituētur	cōnstituitur	constituātur
9. they were being placed	pōnēbant	pōnēbuntur	pōnēbantur
10. you all were being tested	temptābāminī	temptābāris	temptāberis

SECTION 72: PRESENT PASSIVE INFINITIVE. Identify the following infinitives as either active (A) or passive (P) and translate the verb.

currere   **A**   **to run**

1. āmittī	____	_____	7. spectāre	____	_____
2. vidērī	____	_____	8. incendī	____	_____
3. monērī	____	_____	9. cūrārī	____	_____
4. audīrī	____	_____	10. scīrī	____	_____
5. relinquī	____	_____	11. persuādēre	____	_____
6. incipī	____	_____	12. trahere	____	_____

SECTION 72: PRESENT PASSIVE INFINITIVE. Identify the following verb forms as either indicative (D) or infinitive (F) and translate the verb.

trahere   **F**   **to drag**

1. sentīrī	____	_____	6. spectāvī	____	_____
2. cucurrī	____	_____	7. cernī	____	_____
3. ārsī	____	_____	8. temptārī	____	_____
4. posuī	____	_____	9. monuī	____	_____
5. dīmittī	____	_____	10. īnstituī	____	_____

SECTION 74: ABLATIVE OF AGENT. Identify in the blanks to the left of the English sentences whether the underlined phrase is a subject (S), ablative of means (M) or ablative of agent (A).

_S_   **The soldiers marched to Rome.**

__ 1. The tree was hugged <u>by Apollo</u>.   __ 6. The Coliseum was built <u>with stones</u>.

__ 2. The god was pierced <u>by an arrow</u>.   __ 7. <u>The emperor</u> rode with a slave.

__ 3. The Trojan Horse was struck <u>by a spear</u>.   __ 8. Actaeon was seen <u>by Diana</u>.

__ 4. <u>Penelope</u> was weaving a shroud.   __ 9. Priam was killed <u>by Pyrrhus</u>.

__ 5. Odysseus was recognized <u>by Argus</u>.   __ 10. Odysseus won <u>with his bow</u>.

VOCABULARY: DERIVATIVES. Write the English word from the list below, derived from one of the Chapter 17 vocabulary words, that completes the following English sentences in the first blank, and write the Latin word from which it is derived in the second blank. The blank for the English word has been divided into individual blanks for each letter for assistance.

castle	epistolary	exercise	ferrous
judiciary	multitude	discern	constitution
current	currency	incendiary	institute
spectacle	tractor	alternate	feral

1. The _____ is a Medieval version of the Roman fort.

— — — — — —   _____

2. Cerberus was a _____ beast, wild and uncontrollable with his three heads.

— — — — —   _____

3. A _____ of Trojans were killed by the Greeks; few survived.

— — — — — — — —   _____

4. Achilles and Agamemnon had an _____ meeting; Achilles would have killed him if Athena had not prevented him.

— — — — — — — — —   _____

5. The gladiatorial games were designed to be a _____, something everyone would want to see.

— — — — — — — —   _____

6. The _____ of the river Tiber is slow and lazy in Rome.

— — — — — —   _____

7. The Romans had to push their plows while we use _____s to pull ours.

— — — — — —   _____

8. The _____ process in Rome took place in the basilicae where court cases were heard.

— — — — — — —   _____

9. The _____ novel is one based on letters exchanged between people.

— — — — — — — —   _____

10. Roman soldiers _____d by marching every day with heavy packs on their back.

— — — — — —   _____

11. The Romans _____d laws to regulate divorce.

— — — — — — —   _____

12. Apollo could not _____ that Daphne was not interested; he was blinded by love.

— — — — — —   _____

13. The Romans used the sestertius for their _____.

— — — — — —   _____

14. The Romans used lead for their pipes; if those pipes were _____ perhaps the Romans would have been healthier.

— — — — — —   _____

15. Ajax or Diomedes were _____s to Achilles' position as best Greek warrior.

— — — — — — —   _____

16. The representative democracy of our _____ owes more to the Romans than the Greeks.

— — — — — — — — — — _____

CHAPTER 18

SECTION 75. DEPENDENT CLAUSES. In English and in Latin (more so in English) many clause words can also be used as phrase words: the Latin *cum* can introduce either a dependent clause or a prepositional phrase; the English 'before' or 'after' can do the same. In the English sentences below, identify whether the underlined word is a preposition (P) or a subordinating conjunction (C). Be prepared to explain your choice.

    __P__   <u>**Before**</u> **the gladiatorial contest, we met at Marcus' house.**

    _____ 1. <u>When</u> the Romans conquered Carthage, they sowed salt into the ground.

    _____ 2. <u>After</u> the consular election, Marius' supporters celebrated.

    _____ 3. <u>Before</u> the battle, Patroclus borrowed Achilles' armor.

    _____ 4. <u>While</u> Priam and Hecuba watched, their son Hector was killed.

    _____ 5. <u>Before</u> Troy was taken, the Greeks came up with the plan of the Trojan Horse.

    _____ 6. <u>Because</u> it was fated, Troy fell to the Greeks.

    _____ 7. <u>If</u> Hannibal had continued to Rome after Cannae, perhaps he would have conquered it.

    _____ 8. <u>After</u> Achilles defeated Hector, he defiled Hector's body.

    _____ 9. <u>With</u> his loyal army, Caesar approached Rome.

    _____ 10. <u>After</u> Caesar had been killed, his killers fled east.

VOCABULARY: DERIVATIVES. Write the English word from the list below, derived from one of the Chapter 18 vocabulary words, that completes the following English sentences in the first blank, and write the Latin word from which it is derived in the second blank. The blank for the English word has been divided into individual blanks for each letter for assistance.

advent	clamor	gaudy	vulnerable
acceptable	amicable	aptitude	disparity
resemble			

1. Achilles was only _____ in one spot: his heel.

    — — — — — — — — —   _____

2. We are accustomed to the austerity of Greek architecture, but it often had very _____ coloring.

    — — — — —   _____

3. A _____ arose when Lucretia's body was brought to the forum; everyone called for revolt against the king.

    — — — — — —   _____

4. The _____ of Hannibal in Italy spelled trouble for Rome but he didn't stay long enough to win.

    — — — — —   _____

5. Cicero had an _____ with words; in fact, he is considered the model Latin prose writer.

    — — — — — — —   _____

6. Roman architecture _____s Greek architecture but there are significant differences between them.

    — — — — — — —   _____

7. The terms of surrender were not _____ to Leonidas and so he chose to fight the Persians.

    — — — — — — — —   _____

8. Odysseus tried to be _____ toward Polyphemus but when the Cyclops began eating Odysseus' men, Odysseus needed to fight back.

    — — — — — — —   _____

9. The _____ between the Carthaginians' and the Romans' dedication to the battle was due to the mercenary make-up of the Carthaginian army.

    — — — — — — — —   _____

CHAPTER **19**

SECTION 77. RELATIVE PRONOUN. In English and in Latin both the interrogative pronoun (chapter 13) and the relative pronoun look similar (in English they are the same; in Latin, they are very similar with minor differences). In the following English sentences, identify whether the sentence contains a relative pronoun (RP) or interrogative pronoun (IP), and identify the case of that pronoun.

The centurion who disobeys will not last long.	**RP**	**nominative**

1. Who saw Caesar's killers? _____ _____

2. The temple which is most visible in the Forum is the Temple of Saturn. _____ _____

3. Laocoön threw a spear which struck the Trojan Horse. _____ _____

4. Did you see the Greek who killed Priam? _____ _____

5. Whom did Aeneas seek in Cumae? _____ _____

6. Whose orders were Brutus and Cassius following? _____ _____

7. The Coliseum staged battles which were very violent. _____ _____

8. Rome is a city which many people visit. _____ _____

9. What did Caesar say when he was killed? _____ _____

10. The dagger which killed Lucretia was held aloft. _____ _____

SECTION 77. RELATIVE PRONOUN. Choose the relative pronoun that agrees with the antecedent at left. (Remember that pronouns only agree in gender and number, unlike adjectives which agree in gender, number, and case.)

Caesar	quae	<u>**quem**</u>	quod
1. sorōrem	cūius	quārum	quibus
2. nāvum	quam	quem	quārum
3. equōs	quem	quī	cuī
4. vulnus	quī	quae	quod
5. gaudiōrum	quod	quōrum	cūius
6. ferra	quae	quam	quod
7. domuī	quī	quae	quem
8. cīvēs	quae	quod	quam
9. lītorum	quōs	quās	quae
10. undā	quibus	quō	cūius

SECTION 77. RELATIVE PRONOUN. Choose the translation for the Latin phrase at left.

Soror quae vertit.... <u>The sister who destroys</u>
The sister who is destroyed

1. Trōia quam frangunt....

Troy which is wrecked....

Troy which they wreck....

2. Rōma quae incenditur....

Rome which is burned....

Rome which burns....

3. Exercitus quī cernitur....

The army which he sees....

The army which is seen....

4. Epistulae quās amittunt....

The letters which they lose....

The letters which are lost....

5. Castra ad quae trahuntur....

The camp to which they are dragged....

The camp from which they are dragged....

6. Ferrum cuī hostis cēssit....

The sword with which the enemy withdrew....

The sword to which the enemy yielded....

7. Prōvincia in quā aurum pōnitur....

The gold with which the province is built....

The province in which the gold is placed....

8. Diēs quā senātus cōnstituit....

The day which the senate decided....

The day on which the senate decided....

9. Proelia quae exercitus spectavit....

The battles which the army watched....

The battles which watched the army....

10. Iūdicium quod multitūdō cernit....

The judgment which the multitude decides....

The judgment which is decided by the multitude....

SECTION 77. RELATIVE PRONOUN. Choose the translation for the English phrase at left.

The horse on which she charges....   **Equus quō concurrit....**
<u>Equus in quō concurrit....</u>

1. The battle line which the sister sees....

Aciēs quam soror cernit....

Aciēs quae sorōrem cernit....

2. Troy which the horse enters....

Trōia quae equus intrat....

Trōia quam equus intrat....

3. Caesar to whom help is given....

Caesar quī auxilium dat....

Caesar cuī auxilium dātur....

Caesar quem auxilium dātur....

4. The ships with which the citizens sailed....

Nāvēs quibuscum cīvēs navigaverunt....

Nāvēs quibus cīvēs navigaverunt....

Nāvēs quās cīvēs navigaverunt....

5. The old man who lacks his memory….

Senex quem memōriā caret….
Senex quī memōriā caret….
Senex quī memōriam caret….

6. The spouse whom the multitude watches….

Coniunx quem multitūdō spectat….
Coniunx quī mutlitūdinem spectat….

7. The house which the fire burns….

Domus quae ignem incendit….
Domus quae igne incenditur….
Domus quam ignis incendit….

8. The cloud which wrecks the sky….

Nūbēs quae caelō frangitur….
Nūbēs quae caelum frangit….

9. Rome to which legates are sent….

Rōma quam lēgātī mittuntur….
Rōma ad quam lēgātī mittuntur….

10. Caesar whom Rome produced….

Caesar quī Rōma effēcit….
Caesar quem Rōma effēcit….
Caesar quī Rōmam effēcit….

VOCABULARY: DERIVATIVES. Write the English word from the list below, derived from one of the Chapter 19 vocabulary words, that completes the following English sentences in the first blank, and write the Latin word from which it is derived in the second blank. The blank for the English word has been divided into individual blanks for each letter for assistance.

estuary	auxiliary	czar	equine
commemorate	navy	sorority (-ies)	effect
frangible	fraction	versatile	alleviate
elevator	levity	propinquity	

1. The embattled general called in the _____ troops to try to help save him and his army.

— — — — — — — — —   _____

2. The higher you lived in a Roman apartment building the worse the apartment: there was no _____ to take you to the top and the danger of fire was greater.

— — — — — — — —   _____

3. Only a _____ of Romans wrote poetry because of the difficulty of making the meter work.

— — — — — — — —   _____

4. The Romans built a _____ only after they encountered the Carthaginians who dominated the sea.

— — — —   _____

5. Pericles' Funeral Oration _____d the dead of the Peloponnesian War.

— — — — — — — — — —   _____

6. Greek letters represent the mottoes of fraternities and _____.

— — — — — — — — —   _____

7. Caesar died at the feet of Pompey's statue, an ironic _____ given their dislike of one another.

— — — — — — — — — —   _____

8. While the roof supports of ancient buildings were very _____ over time, the stone walls and foundations remained strong and unbreakable.

— — — — — — — —   _____

9. The Romans were skilled horsemen but their rivals in _____ skill were the Scythians.

— — — — —   _____

10. Ovid infused his poetry with a dark _____ that often was at odds with its serious subject matter.

— — — — —   _____

11. The Roman *gladius* was more _____ than the Gallic broad sword, good mainly for impressive looking but ineffective-in-close-quarters brandishing.

— — — — — — — —   _____

12. The ancient Roman port city of Ostia was located in the _____ of the river Tiber, which has since silted in.

— — — — — —   _____

13. At the end of a trilogy of Greek tragedies was a satyr play, a light-hearted play to _____ the depressing _____ of the tragedies.

— — — — — — — —   _____

— — — — — —   _____

14. Maecenas was Augustus' _____ of literary and artistic matters; he oversaw them all.

— — — —   _____

CHAPTER **20**

SECTION 80: PERFECT PASSIVE INDICATIVE. Form the perfect passive indicative of the specified verb using the pronoun in parentheses as the subject, and then translate the verb.

vertō, -ere (vōs)	**versī estis**	**you all were turned**
1. vītō, -āre (nōs)	_____	_____
2. aperiō, -īre (eae)	_____	_____
3. condō, -ere (ea)	_____	_____
4. frangō, -ere (tū)	_____	_____
5. accipiō, -ere (eī)	_____	_____
6. canō, -ere (ego)	_____	_____
7. conficiō, -ere (is)	_____	_____
8. cupiō, -ere (vōs)	_____	_____
9. caedō, -ere (eae)	_____	_____
10. cōnservō, -āre (is)	_____	_____

SECTION 81: PLUPERFECT PASSIVE INDICATIVE. Identify in the blanks to the left the verbs in the following English sentences as either perfect (PF) or pluperfect (PT). If there is more than one verb, more than one blank will be provided.

__PF__   **The consul has been in office for one year.**

_____ _____ 1. Gaul had been conquered by Caesar before he returned to Rome.

_____ 2. 117 poems have been written by Catullus.

_____ 3. The lost standard has been retrieved by the Romans.

_____ 4. Patroclus had been allowed to borrow Achilles' armor.

_____ 5. Marriage had been foresworn by Daphne.

_____ 6. The Pantheon was rebuilt by Hadrian.

_____ 7. Caesar has been seduced by Cleopatra.

_____ 8. The Forum had been drained by the Cloaca Maxima.

_____ _____ 9. The Punic Wars were fought because Aeneas had abandoned Dido.

_____ 10. Greek comedies have been imitated by Plautus and Terence.

SECTION 81: PLUPERFECT PASSIVE INDICATIVE. Translate the following verb forms into English.

crētus erat   **he had been seen**

1. caesī erant   _____

2. cōnservātī erāmus   _____

3. apertum erat   _____

4. condita erant   _____

5. versa eram   _____

6. accepta erat   _____

7. vītāta erās   _____

8. cupītae erant   _____

9. fractus eram   _____

10. cantae erāmus   _____

SECTIONS 80-82: PERFECT, PLUPERFECT, FUTURE PERFECT PASSIVE INDICATIVE. Translate the following verb forms into Latin.

it will have been produced   **effectum erit**

1. she had been received   _____

2. all of you women were saved   _____

3. I will have been sung of   _____

4. those things had been broken   _____

5. he was watched   _____

6. it has been set fire to   _____

7. she was avoided   _____

8. it will have been opened   _____

9. those men were killed   _____

10. we had been wanted   _____

SECTIONS 80-82: PERFECT, PLUPERFECT, FUTURE PERFECT PASSIVE INDICATIVE. Change the voice of the following verb forms.

accēpit   **acceptus / -a est**

1. cantus erat   _____

2. vītāta sunt   _____

3. aperuerunt   _____

4. effēcerō   _____

5. frēgerās   _____

6. acceptī erant   _____

7. crēta est   _____

8. tractī sumus   _____

9. incenderint   _____

10. spectāvimus   _____

SECTION 83: PERFECT PASSIVE INFINITIVE. Identify the tense and voice of the following infinitive forms and translate them.

āmittere	present	active	to lose
1. vītārī	_____	_____	_____
2. conditum esse	_____	_____	_____
3. cupīvisse	_____	_____	_____
4. aperīre	_____	_____	_____
5. acceptum esse	_____	_____	_____
6. cōnficī	_____	_____	_____
7. incēnsum esse	_____	_____	_____
8. īnstitūtum esse	_____	_____	_____
9. āmittī	_____	_____	_____
10. spectāvisse	_____	_____	_____

VOCABULARY: DERIVATIVES. Write the English word from the list below, derived from one of the Chapter 20 vocabulary words, that completes the following English sentences in the first blank, and write the Latin word from which it is derived in the second blank. The blank for the English word has been divided into individual blanks for each letter for assistance.

authority	chisel	incision	significance	insomnia	virile
aperture	charm	recant	abscond	recondite	conserve
cupidity	inevitable	savage	interim		

1. Athena killed Ajax for _____ing with her statue.

— — — — — —   _____

2. Pygmalion the sculptor used his _____ to make his block of stone look so life-like.

— — — — — —   _____

3. Apollo tried everything to woo Daphne: aggression, self-aggrandizement, even _____.

— — — — —   _____

4. Cupid did not suffer from _____ but when Psyche's candle dripped wax on him, he woke up.

— — — — — — — —   _____

5. Achilles withdrew from the Trojan War; in the _____ the Trojans beat the Greeks back to their ships.

— — — — — — —   _____

6. An _____ on the skull that the archaeologist found indicated a sword blow to the head.

— — — — — — —   _____

7. Midas' _____ caused him trouble: everything turned to gold, including his daughter and food.

— — — — — — —   _____

8. Atalanta couldn't _____ any energy when she was leaving the track to chase golden apples.

— — — — — — —   _____

9. To photograph the Coliseum at night, your camera's _____ should be increased to let in more light.

— — — — — — —   _____

10. Proconsuls rule provinces with the _____ of the consul in Rome.

— — — — — — — —   _____

11. Its appearance on Augustus Prima Porta, perhaps Augustus' most important portrait statue, indicated the _____ of the return of the standards from the Parthians.

— — — — — — — — — — —   _____

12. Once Cicero was placed on the list of proscriptions, he could not _____ what he said about Marc Antony and save his life.

— — — — —   _____

13. A mark of the neoteric poets was _____ knowledge of mythology to pepper their poetry with obscure references and stories.

— — — — — — — —   _____

14. When Hector killed Achilles' best friend Patroclus, his death became _____.

— — — — — — — —   _____

15. The Romans erroneously viewed the Gauls as _____s, an uncultured and barbaric people.

— — — — —   _____

16. Athena and Diana were goddesses marked by their _____ nature; they eschewed many of the activities associated with being a woman.

— — — — — —   _____

CHAPTER 21

SECTION 85: IRREGULAR VERBS – VOLŌ, NŌLŌ, MĀLŌ. Translate the following Latin forms into English.

māvīs   **you prefer**

1. nōlunt	_____	11. mālumus	_____
2. vult	_____	12. voluērunt	_____
3. nōlō	_____	13. māvult	_____
4. volumus	_____	14. nōlle	_____
5. nōlī	_____	15. vīs	_____
6. nōluit	_____	16. volunt	_____
7. velle	_____	17. nōlīte	_____
8. malunt	_____	18. māluī	_____
9. nōn vult	_____	19. mālle	_____
10. volō	_____	20. nōluerunt	_____

SECTION 86: NEGATIVE COMMANDS WITH NŌLŌ. Choose the correct translation of the Latin verbs at left (most are commands but not all are).

nōlī canere   sing   <u>don't sing</u>

1. nōlī iubēre	I didn't want to order	don't order [sing.]
2. postulāte	demand [pl.]	don't demand [pl.]
3. nōluī cōgere	I didn't want to force	don't force [sing.]
4. aperī	open [sing.]	I opened
5. voluī vīvere	don't live	I wanted to live
6. nōlīte caedere	don't kill [pl.]	don't kill [sing.]
7. vīve	don't live [sing.]	live [sing.]
8. nōlī sinere	don't allow [sing.]	don't allow [pl.]
9. iubēte	order [pl.]	order [sing.]
10. nōlīte postulāre	don't demand [sing.]	don't demand [pl.]

SECTION 87: NOUN CLAUSE, OBJECTIVE INFINITIVE. Identify in the blank to the left the following English sentences as containing a complementary infinitive (C) or an objective infinitive (O). Review the differences on p.162 of your textbook if necessary.

__C__   Caesar wanted to rule Rome.

_____ 1. Augustus forced his daughter to leave.

_____ 2. Catullus wanted Lesbia to love him.

_____ 3. Catullus wanted to be with Lesbia.

_____ 4. Agamemnon demanded Achilles' girl to be given to him.

_____ 5. Laocoön warned the Trojans not to admit the Trojan Horse.

_____ 6. Laocoön warned not to trust the Greeks.

_____ 7. Augustus did not allow Ovid to return to Rome.

_____ 8. Apollo forced Daphne to flee.

_____ 9. Jupiter preferred to hide his consorts from Juno.

_____ 10. Creon ordered Medea not to cross him.

VOCABULARY: DERIVATIVES. Write the English word from the list below, derived from one of the Chapter 21 vocabulary words, that completes the following English sentences in the first blank, and write the Latin word from which it is derived in the second blank. The blank for the English word has been divided into individual blanks for each letter for assistance.

dolorous	ammunition	immoral	morose
enunciate	principal	servile	cogent
postulation	veto	convivial	victuals
benevolence	malevolence	voluntary	

1. Service in the early Roman army was not _____; all who could afford armor had to serve.

— — — — — — — —   _____

2. A _____ factor in Rome's fall was the over-extending of the size of the empire.

— — — — — — — —   _____

3. Achilles showed _____ to Hector after his death; he desecrated his body.

— — — — — — — — — —   _____

4. It is only _____ why Ovid was exiled; he simply tells us that a carmen and crimen caused it.

— — — — — — — — — —   _____

5. Catullus wrote a poem about Calvus who was not able to _____ the letter 'h'.

_ _ _ _ _ _ _ _   _____

6. Ovid's connection to Augustus' granddaughter is a _____, if unknown, reason for his exile.

_ _ _ _ _ _   _____

7. Roman soldiers carried _____ with them to keep them sustained over long marches.

_ _ _ _ _ _ _ _   _____

8. Vergil's onerous poetry, especially the *Aeneid*, seems to paint him as somewhat _____.

_ _ _ _ _   _____

9. Iliad 5 contains perhaps one of the most _____ scenes in all of literature: when Hector leaves his wife and child to go to battle.

_ _ _ _ _ _ _   _____

10. Augustus attempted to fight the _____ behavior of Rome by promoting values and religion.

_ _ _ _ _ _   _____

11. Catullus used his poetry as _____ against those he disliked.

_ _ _ _ _ _ _ _   _____

12. Baucis and Philemon welcomed the gods with _____, even trying to kill their only goose for them.

_ _ _ _ _ _ _ _ _ _   _____

13. The suitors maintained a _____ atmosphere, until Odysseus returned, even though they were being rude to Penelope and Telemachus.

_ _ _ _ _ _ _ _   _____

14. Roman slaves could buy their freedom; they did not have to be _____ forever.

_ _ _ _ _ _   _____

15. If the Trojans had _____ed the plan of Nisus and Euryalus, they would not have been killed behind enemy lines.

_ _ _ _   _____

CHAPTER 22

SECTION 88: INFINITIVE FORMS. Identify the tense and voice of the following infinitive forms.

postulāvisse	perfect	active
	tense	voice

1. nescīrī _____ _____

2. spērātum esse _____ _____

3. cōgitāre _____ _____

4. negātūrum esse _____ _____

5. iūssisse _____ _____

6. vetitum esse _____ _____

7. ostendī _____ _____

8. respondērī _____ _____

9. trādere _____ _____

10. condidisse _____ _____

11. caesūrum esse _____ _____

12. apertum esse _____ _____

13. cōnservātūrum esse _____ _____

14. canī _____ _____

15. cupere _____ _____

SECTION 88: INFINITIVE FORMS. Change the voice of the following infinitive forms, maintaining the tense, and translate the new form.

iubēre	iubērī	to be ordered

1. respondisse _____ _____

2. spērātūrum esse _____ _____

3. ostendere _____ _____

4. putātum esse _____ _____

5. negārī _____ _____

6. trādidisse _____ _____

7. sītum īrī _____ _____

8. cōgitāre _____ _____

9. nescītum esse _____ _____

10. gaudēre _____ _____

SECTION 89: NOUN CLAUSE – INDIRECT STATEMENT. Choose the correct translation for the Latin sentences at left.

Videt servum canere.   **She sees the servant singing.**
     <u>She sees that the servant is singing.</u>

1. Soror dīcit Graecōs Trōiam frangere.   The sister says to the Greeks to destroy Troy.
     The sister says that the Greeks destroy Troy.

2. Caesar scit auxilium advenīre.   Caesar knows that help is arriving.
     Caesar knows help to arrive.

3. Līberī negant se gaudēre.   The children deny to be glad.
     The children deny that they are glad.

4. Prīnceps spērat fātum vītārī.   The leader hopes to avoid his fate.
     The leader hopes that his fate is avoided.

5. Exercitus respondet prīncipem vīvere.   The army responds to the living leader.
     The army responds that its leader lives.

6. Multitūdō putat mōrēs cōnservārī debēre.   The multitude thinks that the customs should be preserved.
     The multitude thinks to preserve the owed customs.

7. Cīvēs cōgitant auctōritātem condī.   The citizens think to establish authority.
     The citizens think that authority is established.

8. Cōpiae crēdunt iter fīnīre.   The troops think that the journey is finished.
     The troops think to finish the journey.

9. Gēns vult caedem vetāre.   The clan wants to forbid slaughter.
     The clan wants that slaughter be forbidden.

10. Hostēs audiunt prōvinciam incendere.   The enemy hears that the province is burning.
     The enemy hears the province burning.

SECTION 90: TENSES OF THE INFINITIVE IN INDIRECT STATEMENT. In the following Latin sentences, identify the tense of the main verb, the tense of the infinitive in indirect statement, and the relationship that that infinitive indicates. (These are the sentences from ex.143 in your textbook.)

Līberī servum equum āmisisse negant.
     present   **perfect**   **before**

1. Virī hostēs arma trādere postulābant.

_____   _____   _____

2. Virī dīxērunt hostēs arma trādidisse.

_____   _____   _____

3. Servus negāvit sē dominum suum cōnfēcisse.

_____ _____ _____

4. Epistula senātuī nūntiāvit Galliam ā Caesare superātam esse.

_____ _____ _____

5. Senēs spērant puerōs mātrēs patrēsque audītūrōs esse.

_____ _____ _____

6. Caesar dīxit sē ducem copiīs fore.

_____ _____ _____

7. Putant id esse aurum, sed nōn est.

_____ _____ _____

8. Poēta dīcēbat montēs verbīs suīs mōtōs esse.

_____ _____ _____

9. Intellegō ratiōnem mentem sed gaudium timōremque pectus regere.

_____ _____ _____

10. Māter facile docet līberōs haec facere.

_____ _____ _____

SECTION 90: TENSES OF THE INFINITIVE IN INDIRECT STATEMENT. Choose the Latin verb to translate the underlined English verb.

Caesar said that <u>he would conquer</u> Rome.   vincere   vīcisse   <u>**victūrum esse**</u>

1. Augustus said that his daughter <u>was leaving</u>.	discēdere	discessisse	discessūrum esse
2. Laocoön says that Troy <u>will fall</u>.	cadere	cecidisse	cāsūrum esse
3. Apollo bragged that he <u>had defeated</u> the Python.	superāre	superāvisse	superātūrum esse
4. Cicero thinks that the neoterics <u>wrote</u> poorly.	scrībere	scrīpsisse	scrīptūrī esse
5. Menelaus reports that Odysseus <u>is</u> ok.	esse	fuisse	futūrum esse
6. Aeneas told Dido that he <u>had to</u> go.	dēbēre	dēbuisse	dēbitūrum esse
7. Jupiter judged that Hades <u>had transgressed</u>.	peccāre	peccāvisse	peccātūrum esse
8. Ovid hopes that Augustus <u>will forgive</u> him.	ignoscere	ignōvisse	ignōtūrum esse
9. Horace wrote that his poetry <u>would last</u> forever.	manēre	mānsisse	mānsūra esse
10. Homer wrote that Troy <u>fell</u> to the Greeks.	cadere	cecidisse	cāsūra esse

VOCABULARY: DERIVATIVES. Write the English word from the list below, derived from one of the Chapter 22 vocabulary words, that completes the following English sentences in the first blank, and write the Latin word from which it is derived in the second blank. The blank for the English word has been divided into individual blanks for each letter for assistance.

articulate	modality (-ies)	exorbitant	adage
cogitation	rejoice	negate	ostentatious
putative	impute	despair	tradition
imprudent			

1. Achilles was the _____ leader of the Greek army despite Agamemnon's higher rank.

   _ _ _ _ _ _ _ _   _____

2. Perhaps the most famous Latin _____ is *Carpe diem*.

   _ _ _ _ _   _____

3. Dido reacted with _____ when Aeneas left her.

   _ _ _ _ _ _ _   _____

4. Hannibal's decision not to march to Rome after the battle of Cannae was _____; he likely could have conquered it.

   _ _ _ _ _ _ _ _ _   _____

5. The Roman literary _____ is influenced by Greek literature with a Roman twist.

   _ _ _ _ _ _ _ _ _   _____

6. Augustus _____d his vision for Rome through his literary, architectural, and political program.

   _ _ _ _ _ _ _ _ _ _   _____

7. The _____ of Roman poetry include epic, elegiac, and lyric.

   _ _ _ _ _ _ _ _ _   _____

8. Many temples, despite their austere appearance now, were in reality _____ and gaudy.

   _ _ _ _ _ _ _ _ _ _ _ _   _____

9. Cupid's effect on Apollo _____d his bragging about his power and strength.

   _ _ _ _ _ _   _____

10. Roman taxes became _____ as emperors spent more and more money.

    _ _ _ _ _ _ _ _ _ _   _____

11. The _____s of Socrates exist only via the writings of Plato, his pupil.

    _ _ _ _ _ _ _ _ _ _   _____

12. The Romans _____d upon the eventual defeat of Carthage, their long-time enemy.

    _ _ _ _ _ _ _   _____

13. The Etruscans and Romans _____d great power to those who could see the future.

    _ _ _ _ _ _ _   _____

CHAPTER **23**

SECTION 91a: INTENSIVE PRONOUN - IPSE. The intensive *ipse* is translated 'himself, herself, itself, themselves'. This is the same translation as the reflexive pronoun (chapter 13). These words have very different functions, but in English they have the same translation. Identify in the blanks to the left whether the –self word in the following sentences is a reflexive pronoun (R) or an intensive pronoun (I).

__I__   The consul himself presided over the senate.

_____ 1. Dido herself greeted Aeneas in Carthage.

_____ 2. Odysseus sees himself in his young son Telemachos.

_____ 3. Aeneas brought the *penātēs* with himself to Italy.

_____ 4. Menelaus saw Helen herself atop the walls of Troy.

_____ 5. Psyche didn't realize that her lover was Cupid himself.

_____ 6. Hades is assisted by the Titans themselves.

_____ 7. Narcissus can only see himself in the mirror of the water.

_____ 8. Hephaestus built an invisible net for himself to catch his adulterous wife.

_____ 9. Clytemnestra herself greeted Agamemnon upon his return home.

_____ 10. Pentheus was killed by the Bacchae themselves.

SECTION 91a-b: INTENSIVE PRONOUN – IPSE, ĪDEM, QUĪDAM. Complete the following charts as best as possible from memory. When necessary, use the paradigms on pp.175-176 for reference.

	ipse	ipsa	ipsum
		singular	
ablative			
nominative			
accusative			
dative			
genitive			
		plural	
accusative			
ablative			
dative			
genitive			
nominative			

	īdem	eadem	īdem
		singular	
genitive			
ablative			
nominative			
accusative			
dative			
		plural	
dative			
accusative			
nominative			
ablative			
genitive			

	quīdam	quaedam	quoddam
		singular	
ablative			
nominative			
dative			
accusative			
genitive			
		plural	
genitive			
ablative			
nominative			
accusative			
dative			

SECTION 91a-b: INTENSIVE PRONOUN – IPSE, ĪDEM, QUĪDAM. Choose the correct intensive to agree with the noun at left.

orbī	**ipsī**	ipsā	ipse
1. potuum	ipsīus	ipsum	ipsōrum
2. nūntium	eandem	eundem	īdem
3. cibōs	quāsdam	quōsdam	quaedam
4. arcēs	eīdem	eaedem	eadem
5. caedēs	eaedem	īdem	eīdem
6. signum	idem	eundem	eadem
7. orās	quāsdam	quōsdam	quaedam
8. crīminum	quōrundam	quōrumdam	quārundam
9. pōtibus	ipsīs	ipsōs	ipsī
10. modō	ipsā	ipsō	ipse
11. līberōs	ipsās	ipsa	ipsōs
12. mōs	quōsdam	quīdam	quibusdam
13. auctōritātem	eandem	eundem	īdem
14. fata	ipsa	ipsōs	ipsā
15. somnī	cūiusdam	quōrundam	cuīdam

SECTION 91a-b: INTENSIVE PRONOUN – IPSE, ĪDEM, QUĪDAM. Make each intensive agree in the appropriate column with the noun at left. When there is more than one possibility, more than one set of blanks will be included.

partem	ipsam	eandem	quondam
	ipse, ipsa, ipsum	īdem, eadem, idem	quīdam, quaedam, quoddam
1. caedem	_____	_____	_____
2. signō	_____	_____	_____
	_____	_____	_____
3. crīmen	_____	_____	_____
4. cibōrum	_____	_____	_____
5. orbis	_____	_____	_____
	_____	_____	_____
6. līberī	_____	_____	_____
7. arce	_____	_____	_____
8. orīs	_____	_____	_____
9. soror	_____	_____	_____
10. prīncipem	_____	_____	_____

VOCABULARY: DERIVATIVES. Write the English word from the list below, derived from one of the Chapter 23 vocabulary words, that completes the following English sentences in the first blank, and write the Latin word from which it is derived in the second blank. The blank for the English word has been divided into individual blanks for each letter for assistance.

recrimination   potion   arbiter   fruition   defunct
perfunctory   ingress   loquacious   compassion   sequel
consecutive   usurp

1. By the time of the Empire, the senate was essentially a _____ organization; it existed but effectively did nothing.

   _ _ _ _ _ _ _   _____

2. Daphne perhaps gave Apollo a _____ glance before she fled into the woods away from him.

   _ _ _ _ _ _ _ _ _ _   _____

3. Thersites became too _____ after meeting with Agamemnon, and Odysseus beat him for his words.

   _ _ _ _ _ _ _ _ _   _____

4. The Trojan Horse was given _____ into the city via the Scaean Gate.

   _ _ _ _ _ _ _   _____

5. The _____ of the contest of the golden apple was Paris; he chose who the fairest was.

   _ _ _ _ _ _ _   _____

6. Medea concocted a _____ to kill Pelias by fooling him into thinking it would make him young.

   _ _ _ _ _ _   _____

7. Zeus _____ed power from his father Cronos, who had _____ed it from his father Uranos.

   _ _ _ _ _   _____

8. Apollo and Diana reacted with no _____ when Niobe insulted them; they killed all of her children.

   _ _ _ _ _ _ _ _ _ _   _____

9. There is no _____ to the *Aeneid* but a 13th book was written in the 15th-century.

   _ _ _ _ _ _   _____

10. Ajax received serious _____s for violating Athena's temple.

    _ _ _ _ _ _ _ _ _ _ _ _ _   _____

11. _____ invasions of Rome by barbarians were too much; the city eventually fell.

    _ _ _ _ _ _ _ _ _ _ _   _____

12. Augustus' plans came to _____; he managed to consolidated the power that Caesar couldn't.

    _ _ _ _ _ _ _ _   _____

CHAPTER 24

SECTION 94: PARTICIPLES. Choose the correct participle to agree with the noun at left.

potum	fidēns	<u>fidentem</u>	fidentium
1. sociōs	incolēns	incolentēs	incolentem
2. cibum	rogātōrum	rogātum	rogātus
3. ōs	patēns	patentem	patentēs
4. exitia	futūrus	futūra	futūrā
5. artūs	gaudēns	gaudentēs	gaudentī
6. līberōrum	negantium	negantēs	negantibus
7. ingeniō	imperantī	imperāns	imperantem
8. crīminum	putātum	putātōrum	putātī
9. orbis	ostentī	ostentīs	ostentōrum
10. mōs	caritūrōs	caritūrus	caritūra

SECTION 94: PARTICIPLES. Use the verb in parentheses to form the three participles to agree with the noun at left.

modum (spērāre)	spērantem	spērātum	spērātūrum
1. ōre (imperāre)	_____	_____	_____
2. sociōs (vulnerāre)	_____	_____	_____
3. servō (dat.; occīdere)	_____	_____	_____
4. nuntiōrum (rogāre)	_____	_____	_____
5. nāvēs (nom.; trādere)	_____	_____	_____
6. ferrī (interficere)	_____	_____	_____
7. multitūdō (negāre)	_____	_____	_____
8. exercitū (iubēre)	_____	_____	_____
9. ignium (vītāre)	_____	_____	_____
10. lūminis (ostendere)	_____	_____	_____

SECTION 94: PARTICIPLES. Translate the following noun – participle pairs. (You do not have to include case in your translation.)

līberī putantēs   **the thinking children**

1. sorōrem rogātūram   _____

2. sociōs morientēs   _____

3. prīncipēs vulnerātōs   _____

4. nūntiīs vetantibus   _____

5. arcī apertō   _____

6. Caesar respōnsūrus   _____

7. equī occīsī   _____

8. nūbe vertentī   _____

9. Rōmae fractae   _____

10. moenibus vītātīs   _____

SECTION 97: ABLATIVE ABSOLUTE. In the following sentences, underline the ablative absolute and write the noun and participle in the appropriate column (the sentences are from or based on ex.155 of your textbook).

Caesar ūnā aestāte duōbus <u>maximīs bellīs cōnfectīs</u>, in hīberna in Sequanōs exercitum dēdūxit.

bellīs	**cōnfectīs**	
	noun	participle
1. Dominō occīsō servus ab urbe cucurrit.	_____	_____
2. Nostrī mīlitēs in hostēs, signō datō, impetum fēcērunt.	_____	_____
3. Audientibus carmen fēminīs virī deōs laudāvērunt.	_____	_____
4. Bellō fīnītō Caesar Rōmam virōs captōs dūxit.	_____	_____
5. Moenibus patentibus, equus magnus in mediam urbem Trōiae trahēbātur.	_____	_____
6. Illō duce, nihil timēbimus.	_____	_____
7. Turbā spectante, prīnceps ipse illīs persuādēre cōnātur.	_____	_____
8. Caesare in Galliā pugnante ducem novum senātus lēgit.	_____	_____
9. Nautīs nāvigāre parantibus uxōrēs cibum parāvērunt.	_____	_____
10. Crīminibus cognitīs, servus ā dominō interfectus est.	_____	_____

VOCABULARY: DERIVATIVES. Write the English word from the list below, derived from one of the Chapter 24 vocabulary words, that completes the following English sentences in the first blank, and write the Latin word from which it is derived in the second blank. The blank for the English word has been divided into individual blanks for each letter for assistance.

ingenious	usher	oral	association
imperative	immortality	occident	patent
interrogation	arrogance	surrogate	vulnerable
proximity			

1. Achilles was only _____ in one place, his heel, and that's where Paris shot him.

   _ _ _ _ _ _ _ _ _   _____

2. Caesar's death _____ed in a new period of political wrangling and propaganda that ended with Augustus' consolidation of power.

   _ _ _ _ _   _____

3. Poor Tithonus: He was granted _____ but not eternal youth, so he never died but continued to age.

   _ _ _ _ _ _ _ _ _ _ _   _____

4. It was _____ that the Greeks maintain their military formation, the phalanx; if it broke, they quickly lost their advantage.

   _ _ _ _ _ _ _ _ _ _   _____

5. Apollo bragged how much better he was than Cupid, but Cupid made him pay for this _____.

   _ _ _ _ _ _ _ _ _   _____

6. The _____ of Troy to the gateway to the Black Sea made it ideally positioned to control trade routes.

   _ _ _ _ _ _ _ _ _   _____

7. Archimedes needed to determine the volume of a crown, and he came up with an _____ solution to this vexing problem.

   _ _ _ _ _ _ _ _ _   _____

8. There was no _____ of Prometheus; Zeus asked no questions before chaining him to that mountain.

   _ _ _ _ _ _ _ _ _ _ _ _ _   _____

9. There was always an _____ component to Latin poetry, unlike today when we read much of our poetry without hearing it.

— — — —   _____

10. The orient, where the sun rises, is a well known term, but less so is its opposite, the _____, where the sun sets.

— — — — — — —   _____

11. Jupiter acted as an unwitting _____ for Athena who burst forth from his head fully grown and fully armed.

— — — — — — — —   _____

12. It seems that Ovid's _____ with Augustus' granddaughter led to his exile.

— — — — — — — — — —   _____

13. The danger of the Trojan Horse should have been _____ly obvious to the Trojans but it was not.

— — — — — —   _____

CHAPTER **25**

SECTION 98: EŌ, ĪRE, IĪ (IVĪ), ITŪRUS. Identify the mood and tense of the following forms of *eō*.

īmus	**indicative**	**present**
1. ībit	_____	_____
2. ierant	_____	_____
3. eunt	_____	_____
4. ībam	_____	_____
5. ī	_____	_____
6. euntēs	_____	_____
7. iērunt	_____	_____
8. isse	_____	_____
9. it	_____	_____
10. iit	_____	_____

SECTION 98: EŌ, ĪRE, IĪ (IVĪ), ITŪRUS. Translate the following forms of *eō*.

īs	**you are going**
1. ībāmus	_____
2. iī	_____
3. eō	_____
4. ībunt	_____
5. ierāmus	_____
6. ībō	_____
7. īre	_____
8. iimus	_____
9. īte	_____
10. iēns	_____

SECTION 99. FERŌ, FERRE, TULĪ, LĀTUS (TO CARRY, BEAR). Translate the form of *ferō* below, change its voice, and translate the new form.

	fertis	you all carry	feriminī	you all are carried
1. ferēbant				
2. ferrī				
3. lātī sunt				
4. fert				
5. feram				
6. tulerint				
7. ferō				
8. tulit				
9. ferētis				
10. fers				

VOCABULARY: DERIVATIVES. Write the English word from the list below, derived from one of the Chapter 25 vocabulary words, that completes the following English sentences in the first blank, and write the Latin word from which it is derived in the second blank. The blank for the English word has been divided into individual blanks for each letter for assistance.

exit	perish	transitory	confer
infer	refer	relate	adequate
community	infelicity		

1. Caesar chose to _____ with a soothsayer but then did not heed his advice.

— — — — — —   _____

2. Orpheus could not look back at his wife until he had completely _____ed the underworld.

— — — —   _____

3. The Christian _____ continued to grow in Rome until it was too large for the Romans to ignore.

— — — — — — — —   _____

4. Orpheus' trip to the underworld was caused by the _____ of his wife; she was bitten by a snake while walking through the grass.

— — — — — — — —　　　_____

5. Aeneas tried to _____ to the dead Dido he met in the underworld, but she would have none of his pity.

— — — — —　　　_____

6. The Roman navy was less than _____ at the outset of the Punic Wars but eventually, with the help of a captured Carthaginian ship, the Romans improved.

— — — — — — —　　　_____

7. Vergil _____ed before the *Aeneid* was finished and asked that it be destroyed.

— — — — —　　　_____

8. Everything is _____; Rome lasted for over 1,000 years (over 2,000 including the eastern empire) but eventually fell.

— — — — — — — —　　　_____

9. Cicero didn't need to _____ his fate when Antony's proscriptions came out; his death sentence was spelled out explicitly.

— — — — —　　　_____

10. Vergil frequently _____s to the *Iliad* and the *Odyssey* in his *Aeneid*.

— — — — —　　　_____

CHAPTER **26**

SECTION 100: COMPARISON OF ADJECTIVES. Identify the underlined adjectives in the following English sentences as positive (P), comparative (C), or superlative (S).

  __C__ **The Roman *gladius* was <u>shorter</u> than the barbarian broad sword.**

_____ 1. The Coliseum was the <u>biggest</u> amphitheater in the Roman Empire.

_____ 2. The *Iliad* has <u>more</u> books than the *Aeneid*.

_____ 3. Nero or Caligula are known as the <u>craziest</u> of the emperors.

_____ 4. The 2nd Punic War is the <u>most important</u> of the three.

_____ 5. Caesar was <u>very surprised</u> to see who his killer was.

_____ 6. Plautus is viewed as the <u>more popular</u> Roman comic playwright.

_____ 7. Terence's plays, however, are still <u>funny</u>.

_____ 8. "These chariot races are <u>rather exciting</u>, aren't they?"

_____ 9. Catullus wrote <u>empassioned</u> poetry.

_____ 10. Horace was a <u>more reflective</u> and <u>less emotional</u> poet.

SECTIONS 100-102: COMPARISON OF ADJECTIVES, DECLENSION OF COMPARATIVES & IRREGULAR COMPARISON. Choose the correct adjective to agree with the noun at left.

pōtum	aptiōrum	aptius	<u>aptiōrem</u>
1. līberī	prūdentiōrēs	prūdentiōrum	prūdentiōre
2. culpam	turpiōr	turpiōrem	turpiōrum
3. canis	ūtilissimīs	ūtilissimā	ūtilissimī
4. amōrēs	gravissimōs	gravissimīs	gravissima
5. sociōrum	īnfēlīciōrem	īnfēlīcius	īnfēlīciōrum
6. crīmen	commūnius	commūniōrum	commūniōre
7. artūs	fessissimus	fessissimōs	fessissimīs
8. nūntiōs	sanctiōrēs	sanctiōra	sanctiōrī
9. mōrī	iūstissimī	iūstissimō	iūstissimīs
10. orbe	apertissimō	apertissimum	apertissimī

SECTIONS 100-102: COMPARISON OF ADJECTIVES, DECLENSION OF COMPARATIVES & IRREGULAR COMPARISON. Make the adjective in parentheses agree in the positive, comparative, and superlative with the noun at left, and translate all three forms with their noun (you do not have to include case in your translation). When a noun ending can be more than one case, the case is specified in parentheses.

exitiīs (longus, -a, -um)	longīs the long ruin	longiōribus the longer ruin	longissimīs the longest ruin
1. cibī (gen.; commūnis, -e)	_____	_____	_____
	_____	_____	_____
2. amōrī (sanctus, -a, -um)	_____	_____	_____
	_____	_____	_____
3. canem (magnus, -a, -um)	_____	_____	_____
	_____	_____	_____
4. sociōs (turpis, -e)	_____	_____	_____
	_____	_____	_____
5. culpam (iūstus, -a, -um)	_____	_____	_____
	_____	_____	_____
6. ōs (fidēlis, -e)	_____	_____	_____
	_____	_____	_____
7. orbēs (nom.; apertus, -a, -um)	_____	_____	_____
	_____	_____	_____
8. moenium (superus, -a, -um)	_____	_____	_____
	_____	_____	_____
9. auctōritās (malus, -a, -um)	_____	_____	_____
	_____	_____	_____
10. equō (abl.; difficilis, -e)	_____	_____	_____
	_____	_____	_____
11. nāvibus (levis, -e)	_____	_____	_____
	_____	_____	_____
12. sorōris (pulcher, -chra, -chrum)	_____	_____	_____
	_____	_____	_____
13. vulnera (ācer, -cris, -cre)	_____	_____	_____
	_____	_____	_____
14. epistulā (similis, -e)	_____	_____	_____
	_____	_____	_____
15. cīvēs (acc.; bonus, -a, -um)	_____	_____	_____
	_____	_____	_____

SECTION 102: IRREGULAR COMPARISON. Translate the following English phrases into Latin in the case specified in parentheses.

the biggest mouth (nominative)   **maximum ōs**

1. more companions (accusative)   _____

2. the highest love (genitive)   _____

3. a worse crime (accusative)   _____

4. bigger circles (ablative)   _____

5. the biggest walls (nominative)   _____

6. the best custom (nominative)   _____

7. a better leader (genitive)   _____

8. smaller citadels (dative)   _____

9. the worst fault (genitive)   _____

10. the smallest dogs (accusative)   _____

SECTION 104: COMPARISON OF ADVERBS. Identify the following adverbial forms as positive (P), comparative (C), or superlative (S) and translate the form.

celeriter   **P**   **quickly**

1. ūtilissimē   _____   _____

2. gravius   _____   _____

3. prūdentissimē   _____   _____

4. longē   _____   _____

5. saevē   _____   _____

6. levius   _____   _____

7. turpissimē   _____   _____

8. sanctē   _____   _____

9. iustius   _____   _____

10. pessimē   _____   _____

11. magis   _____   _____

12. tristissimē   _____   _____

13. optimē   _____   _____

14. magnopere   _____   _____

15. fēlīciter   _____   _____

VOCABULARY: DERIVATIVES. Write the English word from the list below, derived from one of the Chapter 26 vocabulary words, that completes the following English sentences in the first blank, and write the Latin word from which it is derived in the second blank. The blank for the English word has been divided into individual blanks for each letter for assistance.

amorous	canine	culpable	delete
resistance	aggravate	justified	sanctity
turpitude	utility	facile	primordial

1. Jupiter had numerous _____ relationships, none of which his wife Juno approved of.

— — — — — —   _____

2. Humans were punished for their descent into moral _____.

— — — — — — — —   _____

3. It could be argued that the Trojans were not _____ for the fall of their city; it was the will of the gods.

— — — — — — —   _____

4. When we make a mistake writing, we use the _____ key to erase it; the Romans scratched off mistakes with a sharp tool.

— — — — — —   _____

5. Roman poets make writing in meter look _____ despite how much work goes into it.

— — — — — —   _____

6. Menelaus' anger at Paris was _____; Paris stole his wife.

— — — — — — — — —   _____

7. Pluto, the god of the underworld, has a _____ guard: a three-headed dog.

— — — — — —   _____

8. The _____ of the arch cannot be overstated; the Romans could not have built what they built without it.

— — — — — — —   _____

9. Juno sent a gadfly to _____ Io, whom Jupiter had changed into a cow to hide her from his wife.

— — — — — — — —   _____

10. Some mythologies have humans originating from _____ ooze, an unknown substance that generated life.

— — — — — — — — —   _____

11. Europa could offer little _____ to Jupiter when he tricked her onto his back as a bull and swam across the ocean with her.

— — — — — — — — —   _____

12. Remus violated the _____ of the *pomerium*, a holy boundary around a city, for which he was killed by his brother Romulus.

— — — — — — — —   _____

CHAPTER 27

SECTION 105: PRESENT ACTIVE SUBJUNCTIVE. Identify the following verbs in the blanks to the left as indicative (I) or subjunctive (S).

__S__ deleātis

_____ 1. dēspēramus _____ 6. nesciātis _____ 11. temperent _____ 16. gaudet

_____ 2. floreās _____ 7. putem _____ 12. interficiat _____ 17. trādit

_____ 3. occidunt _____ 8. iubeāmus _____ 13. accidet _____ 18. cōgam

_____ 4. ostendat _____ 9. condō _____ 14. cōgitēmus _____ 19. aperit

_____ 5. neglegāmus _____ 10. frangat _____ 15. negās _____ 20. vetēs

SECTIONS 105, 106, & 107: PRESENT ACTIVE, PERFECT ACTIVE SUBJUNCTIVE & SUBJUNCTIVE OF SUM. Change the mood of the following verbs, either from the indicative to the subjunctive or the subjunctive to the indicative (assume that any –eri- forms are perfect subjunctive).

sītis estis

1. temperat _____ 9. dēspērem _____

2. acciderit _____ 10. occidās _____

3. flōreāmus _____ 11. negāvērunt _____

4. imperētis _____ 12. trādidimus _____

5. interficiunt _____ 13. cōgitāverim _____

6. est _____ 14. nescīmus _____

7. rogent _____ 15. fuerītis _____

8. patent _____

SECTION 108: INDEPENDENT USES OF THE SUBJUNCTIVE. Choose the Latin verb that translates the underlined English verb. (Refer to p.216 of your textbook to review the different translations of independent uses of the subjunctive.)

Let's all <u>read</u> Vergil! legimus <u>legamus</u> legemus

1. <u>I hope that</u> Rome <u>escapes</u> Hannibal utinam fugiat utinam fugit utinam fugiet

2. <u>May</u> Caesar <u>proceed</u> to Gaul. se confert se conferet se conferat

3. <u>Let</u> the people <u>come</u> to the games. veniat utinam veniat nē veniat

4. <u>Let</u> them <u>build</u> their own camp. aedificant utinam aedificent aedificent

5. What <u>should</u> Octavian <u>do</u>? nē faciat nōn faciat faciat

6. <u>I hope that</u> Rome <u>doesn't fall</u>. nōn cadit nōn cadet nē cadat

7. Let Pluto <u>not hold</u> Persephone. utinam teneat nōn teneat nē teneat

8. <u>Let's meet</u> in the Forum. conveniant ne conveniāmus conveniāmus

9. What <u>should</u> we <u>see</u> next? videāmus utinam videāmus nē videāmus

10. <u>May</u> everyone <u>not ignore</u> the gods. nē neglegent nōn neglegent nē neglegant

VOCABULARY: DERIVATIVES. Write the English word from the list below, derived from one of the Chapter 27 vocabulary words, that completes the following English sentences in the first blank, and write the Latin word from which it is derived in the second blank. The blank for the English word has been divided into individual blanks for each letter for assistance.

glorify	motion	accident	desperate
flourish	exhortation	negligent	temperamental
temperature	beatific	erect	

1. Saints are often described as having _____ faces upon their death.

— — — — — — —   _____

2. Augustus _____ed great buildings throughout the city of Rome.

— — — — —   _____

3. The emperors wanted to _____ themselves to strengthen their rule.

— — — — — — —   _____

4. Under Augustus literature and the arts _____ed because of his patronage.

— — — — — — —   _____

5. The _____ in Brittania is much colder than in Rome.

— — — — — — — — —   _____

6. I imagine that Roman legionaries required encouragement and _____ to keep marching.

— — — — — — — — —   _____

7. It was not an _____ when Servius Tullius was run over by a chariot; his daughter did it.

— — — — — — —   _____

8. The gods could be _____; you never quite know what mood they will be in.

— — — — — — — — — — — —   _____

9. Apollo was _____ for Daphne but could not have her.

— — — — — — — —   _____

10. In ancient Rome, if you were _____ in your studies, your teacher would strike you.

— — — — — — — —   _____

11. The _____ of the ship put the sailors to sleep.

— — — — — —   _____

CHAPTER **28**

SECTION 109 - 111: IMPERFECT, PLUPERFECT ACTIVE SUBJUNCTIVE AND SUBJUNCTIVE OF SUM. Identify the following verbs in the blanks to the left as infinitive (I) or subjunctive (S).

__S__ **imperārem**

_____ 1. bibere	_____ 8. spērāvissem	_____ 15. patēre
_____ 2. appropinquāvisset	_____ 9. canerētis	_____ 16. essēmus
_____ 3. temperāre	_____ 10. esse	_____ 17. gaudērent
_____ 4. vulnerārent	_____ 11. tremerēmus	_____ 18. nescīre
_____ 5. interfēcisse	_____ 12. acciderētis	_____ 19. cecīdisse
_____ 6. cōgitāvissent	_____ 13. incolere	_____ 20. condidissēs
_____ 7. fuisse	_____ 14. occiderem	

SECTION 109 - 111: IMPERFECT, PLUPERFECT ACTIVE SUBJUNCTIVE AND SUBJUNCTIVE OF SUM. Change the mood of the following verbs, from either indicative to subjunctive or subjunctive to indicative.

florēbās   **florērēs**

1. imperāvisset   _____

2. erāmus   _____

3. rogārent   _____

4. acciderāmus   _____

5. approprinquat   _____

6. biberētis   _____

7. tollebant   _____

8. occideram   _____

9. vulnerāvissēs   _____

10. fuerat   _____

SECTION 109 - 111: IMPERFECT, PLUPERFECT ACTIVE SUBJUNCTIVE AND
SUBJUNCTIVE OF SUM. Form the imperfect and pluperfect subjunctive of the following
verbs using the pronoun in parentheses as the subject.

bibō, -ere (tū)   **biberēs**   **bibissēs**

1. cōgō, -ere (is)   _____   _____

2. vetō, -āre (nōs)   _____   _____

3. iubeō, -ēre (ego)   _____   _____

4. frangō, -ere (eī)   _____   _____

5. cupiō, -ere (vōs)   _____   _____

6. nesciō, -īre (eae)   _____   _____

7. negō, -āre (nōs)   _____   _____

8. pateō, -ēre (ea)   _____   _____

9. vulnerō, -āre (tū)   _____   _____

10. tollō, -ere (ego)   _____   _____

SECTION 113: TENSES IN DEPENDENT USES OF THE SUBJUNCTIVE - SEQUENCE
OF TENSES. Identify the time relationship that each subjunctive verb indicates.

flōrēret   **same time / after**

1. accidissent   _____   6. approprinquārem   _____

2. occīdāmus   _____   7. resisterent   _____

3. sustulerint   _____   8. incolās   _____

4. vulnerāvissem _____   9. temperēmus   _____

5. interfēcerim   _____   10. gaudeātis   _____

SECTION 114: DEPENDENT USES OF THE SUBJUNCTIVE – PURPOSE CLAUSE.
Translate the following college mottoes that contain purpose clauses (those that begin with *ut*
should be read with some introductory clause before them, e.g. 'Attend this university to…').

Cognosce ut prōsīs. *[Brevard College (Brevard, NC) Motto]*
    [prōsum, prōdesse. to be useful]
Ut omnēs tē cognoscant. *[Niagara University (NY) Motto]*

Ut vītam habeant. *[University of Leicester (UK) Motto]*

Surgō ut prōsim. *[Bradford College (Haverhill, MA; closed in 2000)]*
    [prōsum, prōdesse. to be useful]
Lūcem accipe ut reddās. *[California State University (Fresno)]*
    [reddō, reddere. to return, to give back]

SECTION 114: DEPENDENT USES OF THE SUBJUNCTIVE – PURPOSE CLAUSE.
Complete the following translation by translating the purpose clauses.

> Multās per gentēs et multa per aequora vectus
> > advēnī hās miserās, frāter, ad inferiās,
> ut tē postrēmō dōnārem mūnere mortis
> > et mūtam nēquīquam alloquerer cinerem.

Carried through many peoples and through many seas, / I arrive at this miserable tomb, brother, / **[1.]** _____ [*ut dōnārem*; *dōnō, -āre* = to give] you your last rights / and **[2.]** _____ [*ut alloquerer*; *alloquor, alloqui* = to address, to speak to] your mute ashes uselessly.

1. _____   2. _____

VOCABULARY: DERIVATIVES. Write the English word from the list below, derived from one of the Chapter 28 vocabulary words, that completes the following English sentences in the first blank, and write the Latin word from which it is derived in the second blank. The blank for the English word has been divided into individual blanks for each letter for assistance.

judicial	punish	solar	vintner
imbibe	tremendous	tremulous	civilian
dire	retaliate		

1. It was common at symposia to _____ wine.

   — — — — — —   _____

2. Apollo was _____ed by Cupid for doubting his power.

   — — — — — —   _____

3. To be an architect in the ancient world required a _____ amount of knowledge and precision.

   — — — — — — — — —   _____

4. The _____ life of the Romans occurred in basilicae where the courts met.

   — — — — — — —   _____

5. The myth of Phaethon is a _____ myth, as it involves him mistreating the sun as it coursed through the sky.

   — — — — —   _____

6. Horace's favorite wine was Falernian, grown in a vineyard south of Rome, though its _____ is unknown.

— — — — — —   _____

7. Cincinnatus, after his successful stint as general, just wanted to become a _____ again.

— — — — — — —   _____

8. After the battle of Lake Trasimenum, the Romans found themselves in a _____ military situation as Hannibal continued to march through Italy.

— — — —   _____

9. Jupiter must have had a few _____ moments when his wife Juno caught him cheating.

— — — — — — —   _____

10. The gods _____d against humans for their bad behavior by sending a flood.

— — — — — — — —   _____

CHAPTER 29

SECTIONS 115 & 116: PRESENT AND IMPERFECT PASSIVE SUBJUNCTIVE, PERFECT AND PLUPERFECT PASSIVE SUBJUNCTIVE. Form the verbs below in all four tenses of the passive subjunctive using the pronoun in parentheses as the subject.

bibō, -ere (vōs)

| bibāminī | biberēminī | bibitī / -ae sītis | bibitī / -ae essētis |

1. līberō, -āre (nōs)

_____   _____   _____   _____

2. iungō, -ere (is)

_____   _____   _____   _____

3. requīrō, -ere (tū)

_____   _____   _____   _____

4. interficiō, -ere (eae)

_____   _____   _____   _____

5. rogō, -āre (ego)

_____   _____   _____   _____

6. morior, morī (ea)

_____   _____   _____   _____

7. occīdō, -ere (vōs)

_____   _____   _____   _____

8. quaerō, -ere (eī)

_____   _____   _____   _____

9. colō, -ere (nōs)

_____   _____   _____   _____

10. mīror, -ārī (ego)

_____   _____   _____   _____

SECTIONS 115 & 116: PRESENT AND IMPERFECT PASSIVE SUBJUNCTIVE, PERFECT AND PLUPERFECT PASSIVE SUBJUNCTIVE. Change the voice of the following forms (while most will be subjunctive, not all will be).

dēspērāverītis   **dēspērātī / -ae sītis**

1. coluissent _____   9. requīsīta erat _____

2. habitātī sim _____   10. quaesīverīmus _____

3. iungerēs _____   11. putāvissem _____

4. ēripiāminī _____   12. nescīrentur _____

5. imperāverint _____   13. iūssī essēs _____

6. occīdērunt _____   14. vetēminī _____

7. rogātī essēmus _____   15. cōgeret _____

8. appellēs _____

SECTION 117: DEPENDENT USES OF THE SUBJUNCTIVE. Identify the dependent clause in the following English sentences (the clauses from chapter 28 are included).

The general ordered the centurion to charge.   **indirect command**

1. Caesar asked Brutus what he had done.   _____

2. Nero ordered Seneca to kill himself.   _____

3. The Greeks went to Troy to recover Helen.   _____

4. Sinon made the Trojans accept the Trojan Horse.   _____

5. After Agamemnon took Briseis, Achilles left the war.   _____

6. Catullus wondered where Lesbia was.   _____

7. Orpheus asked Hades to release his wife.   _____

8. Dido was so distraught that she killed herself.   _____

9. Romulus told Remus not to desecrate the pomerium.   _____

10. Apollo inquired whether Daphne knew who he was.   _____

124 | P a g e

SECTION 118: FORMS OF FIŌ, FĪERĪ, FACTUS. Identify the mood and tense of the following forms of *fiō*.

fīēbātis   **indicative**   **imperfect**

1. fīunt   _____   _____

2. fīet   _____   _____

3. fīerī   _____   _____

4. factus est   _____   _____

5. fīat   _____   _____

6. fīēbānt   _____   _____

7. fierem   _____   _____

8. fit   _____   _____

9. factī essent   _____   _____

10. fīēbat   _____   _____

VOCABULARY: DERIVATIVES. Write the English word from the list below, derived from one of the Chapter 29 vocabulary words, that completes the following English sentences in the first blank, and write the Latin word from which it is derived in the second blank. The blank for the English word has been divided into individual blanks for each letter for assistance.

appellation   colonist   fiat   habitation
liberate   miraculous   imprecation   query
conjunction   latitude

1. Orpheus' removal of Eurydice from the underworld would have been _____; no one does that.

— — — — — — — — — —   _____

2. The Greeks commonly sent _____s to other lands because there was not enough in Greece.

— — — — — — —   _____

3. Dido uttered _____s against Aeneas and his descendants as a curse upon them.

— — — — — — — — — — —   _____

4. Hercules _____d Theseus from the underworld where Hades had trapped him.

— — — — — — —   _____

5. At the end of the *Aeneid*, Zeus utters a _____ that the Trojans be allowed to settle in Italy.

— — — —   _____

6. The _____ of Romulus supposedly survives; you can visit its remains (six holes) on the Palatine Hill in Rome.

— — — — — — — —   _____

7. Polysyndeton is an abundance of _____s, words that join other words.

— — — — — — — — —   _____

8. It is a pressing question whether Augustus gave his writers _____ to write what they wanted.

— — — — — — —   _____

9. Odysseus' _____ of Penelope regarding their bed pleased him; she had responded correctly.

— — — — —   _____

10. Roman authors are known by different _____s; sometimes their last name, sometimes their nickname.

— — — — — — — — —   _____

CHAPTER 30

SECTIONS 119: SUBJUNCTIVE OF POSSUM. Identify the mood and tense of the following forms of *possum*. Any form with two possibilities will be given two sets of blanks.

possītis	subjunctive	present
1. possēmus	_____	_____
2. potuisset	_____	_____
3. possint	_____	_____
4. possunt	_____	_____
5. possent	_____	_____
6. posse	_____	_____
7. potuerunt	_____	_____
8. potuerint	_____	_____
	_____	_____
9. possīmus	_____	_____
10. potuissent	_____	_____

SECTION 120: CLAUSES OF FEARING. Identify in the following English sentences whether the dependent clause is an indirect command (IC) or a fearing clause (FC), and identify whether the underlined word would be translated *ut* or *nē* in Latin.

Caesar ordered his troops <u>to</u> attack.   IC   ut

1. Daphne was afraid <u>that</u> Apollo would catch her.   _____ _____

2. Augustus feared <u>that</u> he would not become emperor.   _____ _____

3. Andromache worried <u>that</u> her huband would die.   _____ _____

4. Achilles ordered <u>that</u> Hector's body be returned.   _____ _____

5. Juno persuaded Jupiter <u>to</u> tell the truth.   _____ _____

6. Jupiter worried <u>that</u> he would have to tell the truth.   _____ _____

7. Hannibal was afraid <u>to</u> attack Rome.   _____ _____

8. Priam was afraid <u>that</u> his son would not return home.   _____ _____

9. Jupiter and Mercury ordered the goose <u>not to be</u> killed.   _____ _____

10. Daedalus feared <u>that</u> his son would fly too high.   _____ _____

VOCABULARY: DERIVATIVES. Write the English word from the list below, derived from one of the Chapter 30 vocabulary words, that completes the following English sentences in the first blank, and write the Latin word from which it is derived in the second blank. The blank for the English word has been divided into individual blanks for each letter for assistance.

opulence   victorious   conspicuous   susceptible
irreverence   simultaneously

1. Nero's Golden House was known for its _____, evident in its name.

    — — — — — — —   _____

2. Ovid's poetry is known for its subtle and not-so-subtle _____ but it likely caused his exile.

    — — — — — — — — —   _____

3. The remaining Horatius brother fled the three Curiatii so he would not have to fight them
    _____; he eventually defeated each of them in single combat.

    — — — — — — — — — — — —   _____

4. The number of obelisks in Rome is a _____ reminder of Rome's interest in Egypt.

    — — — — — — — — —   _____

5. _____ generals, under very specific circumstances, could hold a triumphal parade through
    the streets of Rome.

    — — — — — — — — —   _____

6. Dido was made more _____ to the charms of Aeneas by the intervention of Venus and
    Juno, the latter of whom wanted them to fall in love.

    — — — — — — — — —   _____

CHAPTER 31

SECTIONS 122-124: GERUND, GERUNDIVE, PASSIVE PERIPHRASTIC. Circle the correct gerund form.

1. probō, -āre: dative singular

      probandī   probandō   probāre   probandum

2. probō, -āre: nominative singular

      probandī   probandō   probāre   probandum

3. probō, -āre: ablative singular

      probandī   probandō   probāre   probandum

4. committō, -ere: genitive singular

      committendum   committendō   committere   committendī

5. committō, -ere: accusative singular

      committendum   committendō   committere   committendī

6. committō, -ere: ablative singular

      committendum   committendō   committere   committendī

7. conveniō, -īre: accusative singular

      conveniendī   conveniendō   convenīre   conveniendum

8. conveniō, -īre: genitive singular

      conveniendī   conveniendō   convenīre   conveniendum

9. conveniō, -īre: nominative singular

      conveniendī   conveniendō   convenīre   conveniendum

SECTIONS 122-124: GERUND, GERUNDIVE, PASSIVE PERIPHRASTIC. Choose the correct English translation for the underlined words or phrases.

1. <u>Mihi ad ēnarrandum hoc argūmentumst cōmitās</u>, sī ad auscultandum vostra erit benignitās. (Plautus, *Mīles Glōriōsus* 79-80)

    a. It is pleasing to me that this introduction be narrated…

    b. It is pleasing to me to argue this introduction…

    c. This introduction is pleasing to me to narrate…

    d. This introduction narrates itself pleasantly…

2. Mihi ad ēnarrandum hoc argūmentumst cōmitās, <u>sī ad auscultandum vostra erit benignitās</u>. (Plautus, *Mīles Glōriōsus* 79-80)

    a. if it is your inclination to hear it.   c. if you want to hear it well.

    b. if hearing it will please you.   d. if you will hear it with kindness.

3. Aestus erat, mediamque diēs exēgerat hōram; / <u>adpōsuī</u> mediō <u>membra levanda</u> torō. (Ovid, *Amores* 1.5.1-2)

    a. I put my limbs that have been rested…   c. I put my limbs that are resting…

    b. I put my limbs that must be rested…   d. I put my limbs to rest…

4. <u>Laudandō concipit ignēs</u>…. (Ovid, *Metamorphoses* 10.582)

    a. He conceived a passion for praising…

    b. He conceived a praising passion…

    c. He conceived his passion by praising…

    d. He conceived his passion to praise…

5. Erat autem conventum inter eōs clandestīnum <u>dē commūtandō sitū littērārum</u>, ut in scrīptō quidem alia aliae locum et nōmen tenēret, sed in legendō locus cuique suus et potestās restituerētur; (Aulus Gellius, *Noctes Atticae* 17.9)

    a. …concerning the location of the changed letters…

    b. …concerning the location of the letters that will change…

    c. …concerning the letters whose location must be changed…

    d. …concerning the letters whose location has been changed…

6. Erat autem conventum inter eōs clandestīnum dē commūtandō situ litterārum, ut in scrīptō quidem alia aliae locum et nōmen tenēret, sed in legendō locus cuique suus et potestās restituerētur; (Aulus Gellius, *Noctes Atticae* 17.9)

    a. in reading   b. for reading   c. with reading   d. from reading

7. nec freta pressūrus tumidōs causābitur Eurōs / aptaque verrendīs sīdera quaeret aquīs. (Ovid, *Amores* 1.9.11-14)

    a. and he will seek stars appropriate for skimming over water.

    b. and he will seek stars appropriate for water to be skimmed over.

    c. and he will seek stars appropriate for water about to skim.

    d. and he will seek stars appropriate for water that is skimming.

8. Nil opus est digitīs, per quōs arcāna loquāris, / nec tibi per nūtūs accipienda nōta est: (Ovid, *Ars Amatoria* 1.137-138)

    a. nor must acquaintance be made by you through nods:

    b. nor will acquaintance be made by you through nods:

    c. nor are you nodding to make acquaintance:

    d. nor must you nod to make acquaintance:

9. Enim vērō illud praecavendumst, atque adcūrandumst mihi. (Plautus, *Menaechmi* 860)

    a. …this is guarding me and taking care of me.

    b. …this must be guarded against and taken care of by me.

    c. …this will guard me and take care of me.

    d. …this must guard against me and take care of me.

10. Dignum est certē dēlīberātiōne, sitne faciendum an sit relinquendum an etiam dēstruendum. (Pliny, *Epistulae* 10.39.2)

    a. …whether it is happening or being left behind or even destroyed.

    b. …whether it is about to happen or is about to be left behind or even about to be destroyed.

    c. …whether it must be done or must be left behind or even must be destroyed.

    d. …whether it must happen or must leave behind or even must destroy.

11. <u>Dūra dūranda, alta petenda</u>. (Motto of New England College, Henniker, NH)

    a. Difficulty endures, while lofty goals are sought.

    b. Difficulty must be endured, while lofty goals must be sought.

    c. Difficulty must endure, while lofty goals must be sought.

    d. Difficulty will endure, while lofty goals are sought.

12. Pariter <u>praecepta volandī</u> / trādit et ignōtās umerīs accommodat ālās. (Ovid, *Metamorphoses* 8.208-209)

    a. rules to fly   c. rules of flying

    b. rules with flying   d. flying rules

13. <u>Eius reī dūcendae grātiā</u> longā ōrātiōne ūtēbātur eximēbatque dicendō diem. (Aulus Gellius, *Noctes Atticae* 4.10)

    a. With grace for leading this situation…

    b. Grace to be led to this situation…

    c. For the sake of leading this situation…

    d. For the sake of this situation having been led…

14. Eius reī dūcendae grātiā longā ōrātiōne ūtēbātur <u>eximēbatque dicendō diem</u>. (Aulus Gellius, *Noctes Atticae* 4.10)

    a. and he will be speaking all day.

    b. and he was spending his day speaking.

    c. and he was spending his day to be spoken.

    d. and he will be spending his day speaking.

15. Parietī eius in bibliothēcae speciem armārium īnsertum est, <u>quod nōn legendōs librōs, sed lēctitandōs capit</u>. (Pliny, *Epistulae* 2.17.8)

    a. …because he acquires not read books but read often books.

    b. …because he acquires books not to be read but to be read often.

    c. …because he acquires books not for reading but for reading often.

    d. …because he acquires not reading books but books for reading often.

16. Dēfessus ego quondam diūtinā commentātiōne <u>laxandī levandīque animī grātiā</u> in Agrippae campō deambulābam. (Aulus Gellius, *Noctes Atticae* 14.5)

    a. …with the peace of my relaxed and eased mind…

    b. …for the sake of relaxing and easing my mind…

    c. …for the peace of my relaxed and eased mind…

    d. …for the sake of my mind, relaxed and eased…

SECTIONS 122-124: GERUND, GERUNDIVE, PASSIVE PERIPHRASTIC. Choose the correct Latin for the underlined words or phrases.

The Romans crushed grapes <u>to drink wine</u>.   **bibendum vīnum**
                                                      <u>ad bibendum vīnum</u>

1. The emperor <u>must be feared</u>.
    a. metuendus est   b. metuendus   c. metuendō   d. metuenda est

2. Daedalus escaped <u>by flying</u>.
    a. volandī   b. volandō   c. volāre   d. volandum

3. Cupid shot Apollo <u>to punish</u> him.
    a. pūnīre   b. ad pūniendum   c. pūniendum gratiā   d. ad pūnīre

4a. Remus must be killed <u>by Romulus</u>.
    a. Romulō   b. ā Romulō   c. ad Romulum   d. Romulum

4b. Remus was killed <u>by Romulus</u>.
    a. Romulō   b. ā Romulō   c. ad Romulum   d. Romulum

5. The Greeks delivered the horse <u>to conquer Troy</u>.
    a. ad Trōiam vincendum   c. ad Trōiam vincendam
    b. Trōiam vincendum   d. Trōiam vincendum

6. A love <u>of fighting</u> was part of being a gladiator.
    a. pugnandī   b. pugnandō   c. pugnandum   d. pugnāre

7. The Pantheon was built <u>for the sake of worshipping the gods</u>.
    a. colendī deōs causā   c. colendum deōs causā
    b. colendōs deōs causā   d. colendōrum deōrum causā

8. Athens <u>must be visited</u>.

    a. vīsitātae sunt   b. vīsitantēs sunt   c. vīsitandae sunt   d. vīsitāre sunt

9. The Athenians abandoned the city <u>to deceive the Persians</u>.

    a. fallere Persās   c. ad fallendum Persās

    b. ad fallendī Persās   d. ad fallendōs Persās

10. <u>Reading Latin</u> is a joy.

    a. legendus Latīnam   c. legendam Latīnam

    b. legere Latīnam   d. legere Latīnus

VOCABULARY: DERIVATIVES. Write the English word from the list below, derived from one of the Chapter 31 vocabulary words, that completes the following English sentences in the first blank, and write the Latin word from which it is derived in the second blank. The blank for the English word has been divided into individual blanks for each letter for assistance.

    voluptuous   commitment   convene   convention

    approbation   probity   reprobation

1. Apollo was a god averse to _____; he was always chasing a different nymph.

    — — — — — — — —   _____

2. One of the prized values of the early Roman monarchy was _____: honesty and integrity.

    — — — — — —   _____

3. Classics organizations of all types hold _____s all over the country all year.

    — — — — — — — —   _____

4. Aeneas' sojourn in Carthage with Dido was met with _____; Jupiter sent Mercury to tell Aeneas to move on to Italy.

    — — — — — — — — —   _____

5. Unlike Rubens' paintings, most Roman statues do not depict _____ women.

    — — — — — — —   _____

6. All of the gods except for Eris _____d at the wedding of Peleus and Thetis.

    — — — — — —   _____

7. Hades' release of Persephone was met with begrudging _____ by her mother Ceres because Persephone would only be on earth for six months of the year.

    — — — — — — — — —   _____

CHAPTER 32

SECTIONS 125-129. Choose the correct English translation for the underlined Latin and identify which of the constructions from Chapter 32 each sentence illustrates. Be prepared to explain your choice.

1. Ut incēpit fidēlis, sīc permanet.
   (Motto of the Province of Ontario)   _____

      a. as   b. so that   c. to   d. because

2. Vēnātum Aenēas ūnāque miserrima Dīdō /
   in nemus īre parant, (Vergil, *Aeneid* 4.117-118) _____

      a. hunting   c. to hunt
      b. hunt   d. having been hunted

3. Sensit, ut ipsa suīs aderat Venus aurea festīs, /
   vōta quid illa velint; (Ovid, *Met.* 10.277-278) _____

      a. as   b. so that   c. to   d. because

4. nīl habeō quod agam
   (Horace, *Satires* 1.9.19)   _____

      a. because I'm doing it   c. to do
      b. which I'm doing   d. so that I might do it

5. Dīcit: sed mulier cupīdō quod dīcit amantī, /
   in ventō et rapidā scrībere oportet aquā. _____
   (Catullus 70.3-4)

      a. because a woman says it, it should be written….
      b. what a woman says should be written….
      c. what should a woman say….
      d. when women speak, it should be written….

6. cui quot sunt corpore plūmae, /
   tot vigilēs oculī subter - mīrābile dictū - / _____
   tot linguae, totidem ōra sonant, tot subrigit aurēs. (Vergil, *Aeneid* 4.181-183)

      a. with miraculous words   c. miraculous to say
      b. to say miraculously   d. speaking miraculously

7. eaque clāde haud minus quam adversa
   pugna subactī Vēientes <u>pācem petītum</u>   _____
   <u>ōrātōrēs Rōmam mittunt</u>. (Livy, *AUC* 1.15.5)

    a. they send Roman orators, with peace having been sought
    b. they send orators to Rome to seek peace
    c. they send orators, having been sought, to Rome for peace
    d. they send Roman orators for peace, having been sought

8. <u>Ut</u> rediit simulācra suae petit ille puellae /
   incumbensque torō dedit oscula.   _____
   (Ovid, *Met.* 10.280-281)

    a. as   b. so that   c. to   d. because

9. <u>Quās</u> quia Pygmalion aevum per crīmen agentēs /
   vīderat, (Ovid, *Met.* 10.243-244)   _____

    a. whom   b. them   c. us   d. because

10. <u>Nōn colere</u> dōnīs <u>templa</u> vōtīvīs <u>libet</u>,   _____
    (Seneca, *Phaedra* 106)

    a. it is not pleasing (to her) to worship at temples
    b. temples are not pleasing to worship
    c. temples are not pleasing to be worshipped
    d. it is not pleasing (to her) that temples be worshipped

11. Nōn ego Myrmidonum sēdēs Dolopumve
    superbās / aspiciam, aut Grāīs <u>servītum</u> mātribus _____
    ībō, / Dardanīs, et dīvae Veneris nurūs; (Vergil, *Aeneid* 2.785-787)

    a. to serve   c. having been served
    b. serving   d. about to be served

12. <u>Habēbis quae</u> tuam senectūtem <u>oblectet</u>.
    (Terence, *Phormio* 433)   _____

    a. you will have someone who cheers   c. you will have someone to cheer
    b. you will have to cheer   d. you will have a cheering someone

VOCABULARY: DERIVATIVES. Write the English word from the list below, derived from one of the Chapter 32 vocabulary words, that completes the following English sentences in the first blank, and write the Latin word from which it is derived in the second blank. The blank for the English word has been divided into individual blanks for each letter for assistance.

illicit   licentious   admirable   anterior

1. Patroclus' devotion to Achilles and the Greeks was _____, although it ended up getting him killed.

— — — — — — — —   _____

2. The vanguard marches in the _____, while the rear guard marches in the posterior.

— — — — — — — —   _____

3. The Roman Empire is popularly seen as _____, characterized by debauchery and free-living.

— — — — — — — — —   _____

4. Ovid's _____ behavior, for which he was exiled, seems to have involved Augustus' granddaughter.

— — — — — — —   _____